Achieve
MORE
By Saying YES to LESS

The business woman's guilt-free guide
to ending the cycle of feeling drained &
burned out by work & life

JOY EVANNS

InnerSight
Books

InnerSight Books
Prior Lake, MN 55372

Names may have been changed to protect the privacy of those whose stories have been told in this book.

Cover & book design by InnerSight Books.
Cover image used under license from zinkevych / stock.adobe.com.
Registered Trademarks as indicated are property of their respective owners.

Disclaimers:
The purpose of this book is to educate and entertain. It is not a substitute or replacement for professional business consulting or licensed psychotherapy. You are fully responsible for your results in your life and business. The author, publisher, and their agents are not responsible for any injury, loss, or claim arising from your use of the strategies found herein. If you have questions or concerns about whether solutions raised by this book are suitable for you personally or professionally, you are advised to hire professional guidance.

ISBN: 978-0692045107

*Dedicated to all those who have patiently
loved me through my discovery of this philosophy
and now my ongoing practice of
living life with S.A.S.S.*

TABLE OF CONTENTS

FOUNDATION

THE S.A.S.S. SYSTEM:

SIMPLE

ALIGNED (TO YOU)

SUSTAINABLE

SYSTEMIZED

WHERE TO GO FROM HERE

GET THE MOST OUT OF THIS BOOK
WITH THE FREE BONUS MATERIALS:

WWW.ACHIEVEMOREBONUSES.COM

You'll receive the companion journal, a recorded meditation to step out of guilt, AND an exclusive invitation to my private facebook community of high achieving women on this same path.

YOU'RE NOT ON THIS JOURNEY ALONE.

GET YOUR BONUSES AND JOIN THE SISTERHOOD NOW.

CHAPTER ONE:

LIFE AS A HIGH ACHIEVING WOMAN

DRAINED. OVERWHELMED. BURNED OUT. OVERCOMMITTED. Exhausted. Stressed. Empty. As high achieving women with full plates, we're pulled in many different directions, and these are experiences many of us dance with everyday.

No matter what we do at work, our volunteer efforts, or with our family, there always seems to be pressure to do MORE. To reach a bigger goal, make bigger income or impact, have a cleaner house, or be a better leader, partner, mom, or daughter. Pressure, so much pressure to be perfect.

Stopping to rest or take care of ourselves can be riddled with guilt. When someone else wants something, we say YES. We grew up learning that putting everyone else first and sacrificing ourselves was our duty as women.

In fact, the only way to relax guilt-free is when our bodies just won't go anymore. We're only allowed to stop when the pain, headaches, fatigue, and other symptoms make it simply impossible to do anything besides rest.

Otherwise, we don't stop. We just keep running even if we're running on fumes. Trying not to let anyone down. Especially ourselves.

We're our worst critic—highly judgmental of our bodies, our work, our relationships, what we say, even our feelings. We often tell ourselves we shouldn't feel about things the way that we do. We know we should exercise and eat better, but that's just another way we punish ourselves for not being perfect.

Balance is an elusive holy grail. Some days, even laughable. "Oh, I slept some. It was a good day."

Family members notice that we're always working, sometimes they even hate our jobs as a result. And we'd love to spend more time with them or even to have a moment to relax alone—if only we knew how to keep our professional world from falling apart while we were doing that. So many people. So many expectations.

: : : : : : : : : : BUT WAIT...HOLD ON A MINUTE : : : : : : : : : :

What a shit-show, right? I mean, I know you recognized the experience I described because we were socialized this way— what I've outlined is the old paradigm of what it's like to live as a high achieving woman.

Here's the thing: the healing of our broken world is dependent on us rebalancing this paradigm completely in our generation. Because women, particularly high achieving women who get stuff done, carry big missions in the world. Women with big missions are change makers. And goodness knows our world needs help right now.

But doing things the old way out of exhaustion and running ourselves ragged isn't the way to this change. The job that needs to be done is way too big.

To be the change the world needs right now, we all need to show up as our best selves with our cups full—having fun, staying joyful and balanced, focusing on service without sacrifice. No one can achieve their mission in the biggest way while they are feeling drained, overwhelmed, empty, and exhausted.

The trouble is we were taught how to work hard and measure up, not how to value ourselves and create life and work that feels meaningful, balanced, fun, spacious, and satisfying.

What I want you to know is that you can achieve bigger goals and fulfill your mission in the biggest way without working harder or doing any more. In fact, you can actually *be successful and do less* than what you are right now *totally guilt-free*—all without studying any extreme time management hacks or trying to pack more things into your day.

Imagine achieving your personal and professional goals knowing you have nothing to prove anymore AND having more quality time with your loved ones, relaxing afternoons reading on the couch, more fun activities just for you—without feeling like a lazy slug. And what if, by doing things this way, you could actually make a much bigger positive impact in the world too.

Seriously. I'm not joking. Would you be interested in learning how to do this? If so, keep reading because it's exactly what I'm going to show you in this book.

* * *

How to Get Results from this Book in 20 Minutes or Less
This book was developed with busy, high achieving women in mind. Yes, you can read and implement strategies from this

book sequentially, cover to cover. But for many that's not a realistic option. For those who need strategies you can roll with quickly, here's how to use this book:

1. Read the first three chapters so you understand the overview of the philosophy and how it fits for you. (This foundational read may take longer than 20 minutes.)

2. Next, look at the Table of Contents and choose one chapter from the S.A.S.S. System that would best support you where you are right now.

3. Flip to that chapter: Read, Reflect, and then Implement.

4. From then on when you return to the book, choose a chapter that seems most relevant to what you need in that moment and Read, Reflect, and then Implement. (20 minutes or less.)

* * *

What's Missing From this Book

I will say the one thing that this book alone cannot provide that's essential to your success in making this shift is community. And when you're working to uproot an old paradigm as big as this one, the only way you can do that fully is standing shoulder to shoulder with other like-minded women. Women who remind you of your value and who you are when you forget. Which is why before you go any further, I encourage you visit my website to get your exclusive invite to my community:

WWW.ACHIEVEMOREBONUSES.COM

I rested and took time to tend to my spiritual needs. This meant I became much more mindful and intentional about how I spent my time, energy and resources. And in doing this I clarified what my values are, what my highest priorities are, and how to make the biggest impact in the most enjoyable way for me with my skill set.

I listened deeply to what inspired happiness and ease within me and let go old belief systems that I had learned from my parents and the culture at large that were holding me back from living in my joy.

* * *

The Results of these Changes

- I made more money, spent less time working, and what work I did I enjoyed doing more.

- I stepped back from burn out and began to feel more energized, inspired, and alive.

- My chronic back pain went away.

- I eliminated resent in my relationships.

I now know that the patterns of over-working and over-committing and doing things that are not in alignment are only recipes for making me sick AND for stalling out progress in my business. I've seen exactly the same in my clients as well.

As you might have guessed, eventually I transitioned from "gift wrapping garbage" to what I do currently which is mentoring high achieving women to let go guilt-free of whatever leaves them feeling burned out and drained as I did. When they shift their focus to what feels energizing and fun, they stay inspired and get even bigger results for their highest priorities. What I will share with you in this book are the preliminary steps in order to begin doing this yourself.

* * *

Don't be Afraid to Get it Wrong

I'll be the first to admit, the content in this book was originally developed from my many failures and everything I learned from them. Of everything I discuss, I guarantee I have faceplanted on all of these concepts before I figured out a strategy that worked better for me. Many of those stories I will share with you. I continue to refine and practice these processes in my own life and while working with clients. Sometimes even I have a day that is a train wreck.

Shifting out of feeling drained and burned out does not depend on you getting it right the first time or even all the time. It only depends on your ongoing commitment to live the life you want, your belief that you are worthy of having it, and your continuous commitment to stand up and do differently in alignment with your bigger vision when you fall down.

I've got your back, let's do this!

REFLECT:

What parts of this chapter did you relate to as parts of your own story?

How would saying YES to LESS support you?

What would you like to achieve by reading this book?

IMPLEMENT:

- Start this process in community. If you haven't yet, visit www.AchieveMoreBonuses.com to get an invite to join the Facebook community and receive the other FREE companion resources to this book. Don't attempt to do this alone—let's do it together!

- Once you're a member of the Facebook community, I invite you to join the conversation and post your answers to any or all of the first three REFLECT questions on the previous pages.

- And finally, what time are you ready to commit to reading this book and reflecting on how to integrate the concepts that inspire you? Put it on your calendar.

THINKING DIFFERENTLY IS
JUST THE BEGINNING.

TO GET DIFFERENT RESULTS
YOU MUST ALSO *DO* DIFFERENTLY.

CHAPTER TWO:

SAY YES TO LESS GUILT-FREE

As girls we never learned it was okay to say YES to ourselves. The vast majority of women in our lives modeled self-sacrifice. We were socialized to take a second seat to everyone else's wants and needs. And now as adults when we don't operate that way, when we put our own priorities out front, we easily punish ourselves from the inside for not meeting social expectations. That's when guilt shows up.

This book is as much about saying YES to yourself and your wants and needs as much as it is a process about achieving more in a sane, healthy way. It's about saying YES to your big vision professionally and your highest priorities personally. That's why having an understanding of guilt and strategies to get guilt-free about any decision are essential to success through this process. Because you won't say YES to the things that support you if you can't shed the guilt about doing it.

The more you achieve, the more opportunities will present themselves. You'll have to make more and more choices about which things are a YES or a NO for you. And if you're getting trapped by guilt now in your choices, the problem will only get bigger as your success grows.

When it comes to time and energy, everyone has a limit. Everything you say YES to means you're saying NO to something else. So if you want to have time and energy left over for you at the end of the day you've got to move past whatever feelings keep you from protecting that time.

* * *

WHERE GUILT ORIGINATES

The first key to getting guilt-free about anything you're saying NO to is understanding how guilt works. Because if you don't know where this emotion comes from you can't do anything about it. The concept I'm about to share with you rocked my world when I learned it from one of my mentors, Jay Fiset.

This is what's going on when guilt shows up:
We have a particular way we want to behave or be in the world on one hand. And on the other hand we have a particular belief that is *not* congruent with that behavior.

This sets up a situation where there is a gap between our conflicting belief and our behavior. Guilt becomes the bridge that fills the gap. It's a way of *punishing* ourselves for an arbitrary period of time because our belief and behavior are not aligned. The payoff is that at the end of that time we don't need to change either the belief or the behavior.

Example:

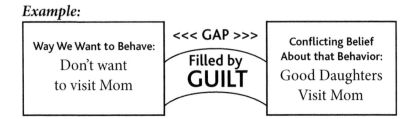

Way We Want to Behave:	<<< GAP >>>	Conflicting Belief About that Behavior:
Don't want to visit Mom	Filled by **GUILT**	Good Daughters Visit Mom

CHAPTER TWO:

SAY YES TO LESS GUILT-FREE

As girls we never learned it was okay to say YES to ourselves. The vast majority of women in our lives modeled self-sacrifice. We were socialized to take a second seat to everyone else's wants and needs. And now as adults when we don't operate that way, when we put our own priorities out front, we easily punish ourselves from the inside for not meeting social expectations. That's when guilt shows up.

This book is as much about saying YES to yourself and your wants and needs as much as it is a process about achieving more in a sane, healthy way. It's about saying YES to your big vision professionally and your highest priorities personally. That's why having an understanding of guilt and strategies to get guilt-free about any decision are essential to success through this process. Because you won't say YES to the things that support you if you can't shed the guilt about doing it.

The more you achieve, the more opportunities will present themselves. You'll have to make more and more choices about which things are a YES or a NO for you. And if you're getting trapped by guilt now in your choices, the problem will only get bigger as your success grows.

When it comes to time and energy, everyone has a limit. Everything you say YES to means you're saying NO to something else. So if you want to have time and energy left over for you at the end of the day you've got to move past whatever feelings keep you from protecting that time.

* * *

WHERE GUILT ORIGINATES

The first key to getting guilt-free about anything you're saying NO to is understanding how guilt works. Because if you don't know where this emotion comes from you can't do anything about it. The concept I'm about to share with you rocked my world when I learned it from one of my mentors, Jay Fiset.

This is what's going on when guilt shows up:
We have a particular way we want to behave or be in the world on one hand. And on the other hand we have a particular belief that is *not* congruent with that behavior.

This sets up a situation where there is a gap between our conflicting belief and our behavior. Guilt becomes the bridge that fills the gap. It's a way of *punishing* ourselves for an arbitrary period of time because our belief and behavior are not aligned. The payoff is that at the end of that time we don't need to change either the belief or the behavior.

Example:

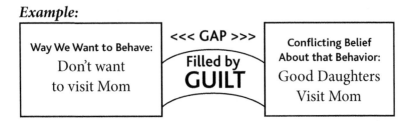

Way We Want to Behave:	<<< GAP >>> Filled by **GUILT**	Conflicting Belief About that Behavior:
Don't want to visit Mom		Good Daughters Visit Mom

What often happens is that we recognize we want to say NO to something but when we think about doing it we begin feeling guilty because of a conflicting belief. We often won't say NO even though we want to in such a circumstance because it elicits too many uncomfortable feelings and thoughts that we don't know how to handle.

The only person who can guilt-trip us is ourselves. When it seems like someone is else is guilt-tripping us what they're really doing is highlighting the gap between our own beliefs and behavior. We create the guilty feelings in the gap ourselves.

* * *

THE SOLUTION FOR GUILT

Experiencing guilt is simply an invitation to change your belief or your behavior. You can do this on your own, but it can be a challenge because we get blinded by our own point-of-view. An outsider's perspective can help greatly.

The best way for me to illustrate this is with a story. One of my clients that was constantly overwhelmed by her to-do list had a volunteer commitment as the president of her state professional association. She wanted to have that time to invest in projects that moved the needle on her business. But she felt terribly guilty and was paralyzed about letting the leadership position go because there was no one else to do it. And so she kept on doing it and doing it and doing it.

Knowing how guilt works, I knew exactly what questions to ask to shift this for her immediately. What she wanted to do was let go of the volunteer commitment. But she had conflicting beliefs that kept her from doing that.

To her volunteering meant she made an impact and she believed good people give back to their community. She also had a belief that good people follow through on their commitments no matter what. And, because those beliefs were not congruent with letting go of the volunteer commitment, the guilt showed up and she got stuck. She was left unable to move forward with what she wanted.

So here's how to get unparalyzed in a situation like this— you have two choices, you change the belief, OR you change the behavior to be aligned with the belief you already have. Most often, the better choice is to shift the belief.

I asked her what impact her business would have on the world if it was running the way she envisioned it. She started listing off all the many ways it would make a difference. She could donate more money, more people would be free from the financial drudgery of jobs they hated, they wouldn't be stuck in poverty, and on and on.

I asked her what impact she was making in the volunteer role she had. She told me, "The last event I planned for the group no one even attended except the speaker."

I reframed the choice, "So if you were to think about this as a choice about where can you best allocate your time resources to make the biggest impact in the world, is this volunteer position the best place to do that?"

She responded, "No, my business is the best place to do it."

I continued, "So is there a bigger commitment at play here than the one you've made to your association?"

"Yes, my commitment to make an impact," she smiled, knowing what was coming next.

I didn't disappoint, "So would you be open to completing this commitment as president of the association now that you see that?"

Glowing and with a big grin, as if the weight of the world was finally off her shoulders, she replied, "Yes. And even if I just used the time to get a manicure, I would be happier." She was now guilt-free and she had joyfully given herself permission to let go of something draining.

* * *

GUILT-FREE SELF-CARE

Sometimes the hardest things to feel good about saying YES to are ones that relate to our own self-care. But when everything about how we've been socialized says it's selfish to take care of yourself it's easy to feel guilty about doing things purely for your own joy and pleasure.

Actually, self-care isn't selfish at all. We are part of a collective network. And even though we often don't see it, everything we do affects everyone else in the web of life. When we're at our best, when we are feeling joyful, energized, and inspired we affect everyone around us with that positivity. And then they in turn affect everyone around them.

The same is true if we are feeling drained, depressed, overwhelmed, and uninspired. Nurturing ourselves in whatever ways bring out our joy and fill our tank is not just a gift of love to us. It's a gift of love to everyone around us and everyone around them. It is a guilt-free way of bringing love to the whole world.

* * *

CHANGING SUBCONSCIOUS PATTERNS:
THE GUILT-FREE SELF-CARE MEDITATION

Old patterns about what it means to take care of ourselves are often so ingrained that responses and resistance happen automatically. So how do we retrain the subconscious part of us? I've found that using a guided meditation is a great way to shift these patterns for good. This way you can more easily stop saying YES to things that leave you feeling drained and start saying YES to ones that restore your energy.

I've included a recording of *The Guilt-Free Self-Care Meditation* as part of the bonus materials for this book. If you haven't already, get the bonuses now. Then you can start using the guided meditation so that you stop feeling guilty and resistant to taking care of yourself in the ways you already know best. Here's the website to get all the bonuses including the meditation:

WWW.ACHIEVEMOREBONUSES.COM

* * *

How to Use the Recorded Meditation

To shift your subconscious beliefs, find a comfortable place where you won't be interrupted. The recording will play on your computer or you can load it onto your phone so you have access to it anywhere. Relax and follow along with the feel-good story about how taking care of yourself and doing what brings you joy impacts the world in a positive way.

Listen a few times a week until you start noticing some shift in how you feel about self-care. If you find yourself feeling guilty about choices that take care of you, that's a great time to listen to this meditation too. This will help you focus on the bigger picture and step into feeling guilt-free immediately.

* * *

Saying YES to LESS Requires Saying NO More Often

Focusing your attention on your highest priorities ultimately requires declining more opportunities that are draining, distracting, or not a fit for you. It's another place that guilt can take over because it involves people.

For such a small word, NO can be a difficult one to say. Why? Because we don't want to hurt anyone. We don't want to disappoint anyone. We want to fit in. We don't want to let anyone down. We want to be liked. This is fertile ground for guilt. Now that you know how to diffuse this showstopper, don't let guilt and other uncomfortable emotions keep you from having the conversations that will set you free.

* * *

WHY USING NO AS A COMPLETE SENTENCE IS A BAD IDEA

Many women have told me that the best advise they ever got about saying NO was that, "NO, is a complete sentence." There's a very good reason why I don't recommend that.

Our core survival strategy as women is building relationships. We're not the strongest or fastest compared to men. So when the shit hits the fan our best strategy is to be connected to others who might help us. So it makes sense that as women we don't want to burn bridges in our relationships. Our DNA is programed with the knowing that relationships keep us safe.

Using the word NO as a complete sentence risks burning bridges because it does nothing to affirm the relationship in any way. This type of statement is perfect for when safety is involved:

- "NO!" (Don't cross the street a car is coming.)

- "NO!" (I'm not interested in having sex with you.)

- "NO!" (Don't touch the stove it's hot.)

In any other circumstance more words will be gentler and more effective in maintaining a high quality relationship. This is another reason why the word NO is a difficult word to say for women, we know intuitively that more words are better. The good news is that most of the time it's possible to firmly set a boundary or decline an offer without even using the word NO at all. Instead, focus on what you're saying YES to and affirming the relationship in the conversation.

* * *

Say NO & Have People Fall in Love with You in the Process
If you're saying YES to LESS you'll have to be saying NO to more things. This is my favorite guilt-free strategy for how to say NO that comes straight from my 6-week boundary-setting bootcamp, *Say NO Like a Pro.*

The process is called the I Love You Sandwich and it's a great way to deliver news that the other person may not want to hear while rarely using the word NO. It works well in both personal and professional relationships, both in written and verbal form. Recipients of this method commonly express genuine gratitude because they feel so affirmed even though the news they've received isn't what they may have wanted.

The three steps of the I Love You Sandwich:

Step 1: The 1ˢᵗ Slice of Bread = An "I Love You" Statement
Purpose: To get them listening

What to Say: With someone who you do love (your partner, parent, or child) you can literally start with, "I love you." Otherwise, begin with a compliment or words of appreciation such as, "I really appreciate all the hard work you've put into this project." Whatever you say it must be true or the person will see right through it. So think of something nice that's genuine however small it might be.

EXAMPLE: "Honey, I love you and the kids."

STEP 2: The Meat = AND + Your Difficult News
PURPOSE: To set your boundary or deliver difficult news

WHAT TO SAY: Beginning with the conjunction AND (not BUT), state the difficult news you have to deliver clearly. Be careful to avoid using the word BUT. If you say BUT, it negates the nice loving thing that came before it that got them listening.

EXAMPLE: "...AND I've realized I need some time alone after work to reset before jumping into being Mom and wife."

STEP 3: The 2ⁿᵈ Slice of Bread = Another "I Love You" Statement
PURPOSE: To affirm the relationship

WHAT TO SAY: Let them know that the relationship is important to you and (indirectly) that you intend for it to continue. You might mention something you're looking forward to or what you're open to instead if you're declining something they proposed. You might suggest that you figure out a solution together. Even though you're declining an offer or making a request they might not be happy about, let them know they are valued.

EXAMPLE: "I'd like to talk about how we can restructure our schedule so that we can both show up at our best as partners and parents."

* * *

LIVING GUILT-FREE IS UP TO YOU
Now that you know how guilt works it's up to you to adjust your beliefs or behavior so you can feel good saying YES to LESS. If you struggle doing this on your own, then get support

from a friend or hire a mentor. That way you'll stay on track with achieving more while living in sane, healthy way.

REFLECT:

What did you learn from your role models growing up about saying YES to yourself (or not)?

Where does guilt get in your way relative to saying YES to LESS?

Think of one thing you'd like to do or have that you have a hard time saying YES to it because you feel guilty or uncomfortable about it. Identify the what you want and the conflicting belief(s) that you have about it.

How might you think about this situation differently and shift either your belief or your behavior so that you're not in conflict anymore?

IMPLEMENT:

- If you haven't downloaded the FREE bonus content with *The Guilt-Free Self-Care Meditation,* do that now: www. AchieveMoreBonuses.com. Put it on your phone so you can access it anywhere. Listen to the recording a few times this week.

- What is one small issue that you will commit to having a conversation about using the I Love You Sandwich this week?

YOU ARE NOT REQUIRED TO
SET YOURSELF ON FIRE TO
KEEP OTHERS WARM.

- UNKNOWN

YOU ARE NOT REQUIRED TO
SET YOURSELF ON FIRE TO
KEEP OTHERS WARM.

- UNKNOWN

CHAPTER THREE:

ACHIEVE MORE WITH S.A.S.S.

OUR WORLD NEEDS WOMEN WITH BIG VISIONS WHO ALSO GET things done. Doing and achieving matters when it comes to shifting what's happening in our world for the better. And yet, the journey to the change we're after is a marathon not a sprint. So if we don't take time to enjoy the trip to the destination, what will we be left with at the end?

Bronnie Ware is an Australian nurse who reflects on her blog and later in her book, *The Top Five Regrets of the Dying,* about regrets people had at the end of their lives based on her experiences as a palliative care nurse. Her patients *didn't* wish they had worked more. In fact, they regretted having worked so hard and not having spent more time with their families.

Further, they wished they had been more of themselves in their relationships instead of who others expected. They wished they had allowed for more happiness, expressed their true feelings, and stayed in touch with friends. In short, they wished they had slowed down and enjoyed the journey with people they cared about instead of focusing so hard on getting to wherever they were going.

The idea of living without regret can actually create more pressure and lead to saying YES to doing everything. Do, do, do, go, go, go. Fear of missing out (F.O.M.O.) is real. Saying YES to trying to be a perfect mom, wife/partner, or daughter, on top of saying YES to your professional goals is a lot for anyone. It's not any surprise this can lead to feeling drained and burned out. And left unchecked, it can escalate to serious health issues.

The other alternative seems to be choosing to sacrifice one area of your life for another. A good example of this is in the movie, *The Devil Wears Prada*. In it, Meryl Streep plays Miranda Priestly, a diabolical fashion magazine editor who is quite awful to her assistant played by Anne Hathaway. Miranda is at the top of her game in her career. She always looks great and despite her mean girl demeanor she seems like she's got it all. Up until when it's revealed that she doesn't.

There's a scene when Miranda is at home on the couch in her grey bathrobe. She looks like she's been crying and hasn't slept. She's not wearing make-up—something is obviously wrong. Miranda tells her assistant that they need to change the seating chart for the upcoming party. Her husband won't be attending and she reveals they are getting a divorce. "Another divorce," she sighs. She worries about the publicity and how awful it is for her daughters.

This is what can happen when a high achieving woman sacrifices one priority for another. One of our greatest fears is that our achievement costs us relationships with people we care about.

So we've got the "do too much of everything until you're drained" option, and we've got the "abandon something you care about" option—who wants either of those??? The good news is that this doesn't have to be a lesser of two evils conversation.

There is a solution that supports both achievement and also doing less: prioritizing the things that matter most like being with people you love, taking care of your health, and having opportunities to play and have fun. The answer I've come to is this: to live with S.A.S.S.

* * *

WHAT IT MEANS TO LIVE WITH S.A.S.S.

A woman who lives with S.A.S.S. is unconventional—a risk taker, rule breaker, paradigm shifter. She deeply appreciates the simple pleasures of life and actively cultivates experiences that inspire, energize, and stir joy. She knows that LESS is actually MORE.

She sets a goal, goes out and achieves it, and then celebrates. She focuses on achieving and acquiring only the things that add value to her life. She balances being loving and generous with others with being loving and generous with herself. She prioritizes rest, play, and quality time with people she loves because that makes life worth living and it helps her productivity at work too.

She questions the status quo and quiets the itty bitty shitty committee in her head. She listens to her own inner wisdom instead of buying into what other people think is right for her. And she builds systems that allow her to leverage her time and receive support. She knows she has nothing to prove to anyone and that she is enough exactly as she is.

* * *

INTRODUCING THE S.A.S.S. SYSTEM

The S.A.S.S. System is a four principle guiding philosophy that enables high achieving women to be more efficient, effective, and productive both personally and professionally. At the same time it creates space for what matters most: quality time with people you love and taking guilt-free breaks for rest, play, and fun. It can help you step back from feeling drained and burned out and achieve more by saying YES to LESS.

* * *

THE FOUR PRINCIPLES OF THE S.A.S.S. SYSTEM

I have found that if you are missing any one of these principles in any aspect of your life you set yourself up to get drained and burned out:

S̲IMPLE
A̲LIGNED (TO YOU)
S̲USTAINABLE
S̲YSTEMIZED

When your choices and activities are congruent with this philosophy you don't need to worry about trying to cram more into your day. Achievement happens more naturally, you stay healthier, and you still have time for what matters most. It's about choosing the goals and activities that make the most impact for you and keep you feeling energized and inspired both personally and professionally.

Each of these four principles is made up of three pillars or aspects that relate more to their specific application. I'll give an overview of all of these in just a moment and will go into a lot more detail about each pillar in subsequent chapters.

The Four Questions:
Quick Decision-Making Using the S.A.S.S. System

Each of the four principles describe things you get to continue to say YES to both personally or professionally. Anything that doesn't fit as a YES, particularly in the first three questions becomes a much easier, "NO, thank you."

Here are the four questions:

1. SIMPLE: Will it keep my life and work simple?

2. ALIGNED: Is it aligned for me? (Are you excited about saying YES?)

3. SUSTAINABLE: Is it personally sustainable? (Does it support my long-term health?)

4. SYSTEMIZED: Can it be systemized?

* * *

Getting into Balance & Staying There with S.A.S.S.

When you're having a challenge with staying balanced it's easy to recognize which principle and pillar need more attention so you can resolve the issue. Take Stephanie for example.

Stephanie is an executive in the tech industry. She worked all hours of the day and often over the weekends. She was chronically exhausted and rarely saw her kids except when they were sleeping. And as much as this routine was normal for her industry, she realized that she was the one setting the standard for her team to follow. Yes, there were deadlines to meet and there were better ways to meet them.

When looking at the S.A.S.S. System, she realized she was out of balance was in two places in the Sustainable principle: "Work in Partnership with Your Body" and "Build in Breaks."

She wasn't listening to what her body needed because she was always tired. She also wasn't leveraging the power of her subconscious to solve problems while she was taking breaks relaxing and having fun. With the Aligned principle she was out of balance with "Invest in What You Value Most" because she was prioritizing her work over seeing her kids.

With this acknowledgement, she adjusted her schedule. Sundays became work-free family day. Weekdays she began having breakfast with her kids. She came home for family dinner every night and instead did some work later in the evening. Twice a week she joyfully took the evenings off to spend with her husband. She stopped feeling tired and the quality and speed of her work improved. Tasks that seemed to drag on before were completed with ease.

Reflecting on the affect the changes had made in her own life she instituted new policies about how late her team could work, required them to take at least one day per week off, and reminded those who emailed her late in the day to spend time with their families.

* * *

TAKING INVENTORY & GETTING STARTED

Using this system requires reflection on what's happening for you, referring to the system, and making adjustments based on what you notice. In a complicated situation, start with what's obvious and work from there. As things become less complex it will become easier to see what else needs to be addressed.

You've probably heard that the easiest way to eat an elephant is one bite at a time. Just start somewhere. Keep making bite-sized shifts that move you closer to being in alignment with the philosophy. Every step is more quality of life for you.

LIVING WITH S.A.S.S.

AN OVERVIEW OF THE PRINCIPLES & PILLARS:

SIMPLE

ALIGNED (TO YOU)

SUSTAINABLE

SYSTEMIZED

LIVING WITH S.A.S.S.

SIMPLE

Simple at the core is uncomplicated. Everything unnecessary has been eliminated—only the essentials in all their glory remain.

Culturally, it is reinforced over and over that it is desirable to do more, be more, and have more—always more, more, more. Over time this chase becomes exhausting and overwhelming because it never leads to the simple experiences we really want: happiness, fulfillment, acceptance, and love.

We've learned to desire, acquire, and achieve things because this is what we think we *should* do not because it leads to any significant increase in quality of our lives. And as we do this we add unnecessary complexity and distraction from what matters most.

With complexity there are many more places where something can go sideways. Complexity requires more time, energy, management, and support. Whereas simple is efficient. It's easy to implement, easy to explain, easy to maintain, and very straight forward.

By eliminating the complex clutter of what doesn't add value to our lives—in our homes, in our work, in our relationships, and in our schedules—we make room for gratitude, appreciation, enjoyment, fulfillment, love, and even rest.

SIMPLICITY NURTURES EFFICIENCY

THE 3 PILLARS OF SIMPLE:

SIMPLICITY WINS

Keeping life and work simple allow you to see and appreciate what matters most. Unnecessary complexity reduces efficiency, confuses people, and undermines confidence. Clutter in your home and office and on your to-do list distract you from your highest priorities. Happiness isn't something you achieve, it's born daily from gratitude for life's simple wonders.

CHOOSE QUALITY OVER QUANTITY

Know when LESS is actually MORE. Managing more relationships and more stuff also require more time and resources. Go deep with people you love, give them your full attention. Collect experiences instead of things. Know that you are lovable and enough just the way you are and you have nothing to prove through achievement. Develop appreciation for what you have. Focus on achieving the next goal because it will add value to your life or organization, not because it's the thing that's next.

STREAMLINE YOUR FOCUS

When you dilute your focus you delay and diminish your results. Spreading your attention too broadly means you won't make significant progress on anything. Intently do one thing at a time and focus on one goal at a time whenever possible. Multi-tasking is extremely inefficient. The more you can tailor your activities to reflect only your highest priorities, the more impact you will make in those areas.

LIVING WITH S.A.S.S.
ALIGNED (TO YOU)

Creating life and work that are aligned to you has to do with the cohesion of mind, body, and spirit. So often we run our lives by other peoples beliefs and rules: what our parents and culture told us was good. It's exhausting when we're doing things that aren't a natural fit for us. Yet we've been playing this way for so long that it's easy to think that these rules belong to us until we examine our inner world more closely.

Listening deeply what's going on in your inner world is at the core of staying aligned. It requires slowing down, honoring your intuition. Giving yourself permission to acknowledge what you really want. Taking consistent action in ways that embody what you really want.

It involves getting all the parts of you on the same page in whatever you're doing, whether that's working late or indulging on vacation or doing a favor for someone. It requires acknowledging the places where you sabotage yourself because your beliefs aren't congruent your choices. And when you aren't experiencing the results you want, starting by looking within to make the adjustment. Getting aligned requires telling the truth—both to yourself and to people you care about.

When you design life and work around what fits well for you it is easy to feel energized, excited, inspired, passionate, and fulfilled. When you're out of alignment playing by other people's beliefs and rules, doing things that aren't a natural fit becomes draining.

ALIGNMENT ACTIVATES ACHIEVING WITH JOY

THE 3 PILLARS OF ALIGNED:

Follow Your Heart & Intuition

We grew up learning that logic is the best way to make decisions and to automatically override both our inner wisdom and knowing in our body. Yet your intuitive nudges give you access to helpful unseen information that your conscious mind could never anticipate. This data can come in many ways and with practice it can help you make the most aligned choices for you. Aligned choices lead to more health, grace, and ease.

Own Your Inner Game

Your beliefs, thoughts, feelings, and actions create the experience you're having. If you want different results that starts with shifting and realigning what's happening for you on the inside. Staying in victim mode or blaming your circumstances on something else isn't the path to getting more of what you want. Until you take ownership of your participation you can't do anything to change it.

Invest in What You Value Most

Take action and spend your time, energy, and money on your highest priorities. If you want a different outcome than what you're getting personally or professionally, start by checking where your investments may be out of alignment with your values. Recognize that it's not possible to invest in all your values at the same time. Attempting to do so will mean you don't achieve what you want anywhere.

LIVING WITH S.A.S.S.
SUSTAINABLE

High achieving women run themselves hard. Most feel pulled in many different directions all at once and sacrifice their own needs for their work and families. Short-term rewards come by doing this both personally and professionally, but at what long-term cost to health and performance?

Sustainable practices are energizing. Feeling drained and burned out happens when your energy is depleted faster than it is restored. At some point anyone will hit a wall if there is not consistent focus on processes that renew energy.

Making time to take restorative breaks to rest, play, and have fun is essential to stay inspired and maintain motivation, productivity, and focus. This requires paying attention to what your body, mind, and spirit all need.

Operating from a sustainable mindset includes practicing being a good receiver by welcoming in support both personally and professionally. Going it alone isn't an option anymore. This requires letting go of control and trusting in your process and the people who support you to do their part. Working at a pace and capacity that fit for you physically, mentally, emotionally, and spiritually over the long-term is also at the heart of sustainability.

SUSTAINABILITY RENEWS ENERGY

THE 3 PILLARS OF S̲USTAINABLE:

Work in Partnership with Your Body

Your body enables your achievement. So listen to what support it needs. Rest when you need to rest, eat when you need to eat, and so on. The same goes for your team. Honor their limits and encourage them to listen to their bodies too. This can be fun, not just another thing to do.

Build in Breaks

Instead of powering through and just working harder, let your subconscious discover solutions while you are taking a break to play, relax, exercise, sleep, and recharge. Make this a regular part of your process. Work a schedule that provides enough time for you to restore yourself, and take work-free vacations so you return to the office with renewed productivity and ability to focus.

Welcome Support

Going it alone is the old paradigm. To achieve bigger things you need to allow in bigger support. Do what falls in your genius zone, the area of your natural joy, skills, and talent where you do your best work. Delegate everything else as often as possible. Surround yourself with friends, colleagues, and mentors who uplift, inspire, and remind you who you are when you forget.

LIVING WITH S.A.S.S.

<u>S</u>YSTEMIZED

Time is our most valuable resource. Everyone has twenty-four hours in a day and once it's gone it's gone. There's only so much that can be packed into any day so developing processes that leverage your time and wisdom are essential to achieving more with less strain.

This is where systems help. A good working system is a repeatable process that delivers a specific desired result. It reduces decision-making while increasing consistency and quality control.

Systems can be designed for both personal and professional purposes. A morning routine, grocery shopping, answering the phone, generating new customers, and tracking existing projects are all processes that can be systemized.

Whether we follow a system once we've created it has a lot to do with whether we enjoy it and how well it fits for us. Structure for the sake of structure is not the goal. Freedom and scalability are what we want.

The best case scenario is when a system can deliver the result you want in a way does not require your personal participation. Then it can be completely delegated to an assistant, family member, or someone else on your team.

SYSTEMS STREAMLINE SUCCESS

THE 3 PILLARS OF SYSTEMIZED:

IMPLEMENT SYSTEMS THAT SUPPORT FREEDOM & SCALABILITY

Focus on developing, implementing, and refining processes that are enjoyable and consistently achieve your desired results. To maximize freedom and scalability, the more you can leverage your own time by designing the system to run without your intervention, the better.

DOCUMENT YOUR SYSTEMS & KNOWLEDGE

A system that exists only in your head doesn't help you leverage support. Documentation ensures more consistent results and enables you to get help more easily. Make sure that you and your team document the processes you use in ways that are easy and enjoyable for someone else to follow.

ALLOW YOUR PLANS & SYSTEMS TO EVOLVE

Things change. Life happens. Markets shift. People grow. Be open to adjusting how you're doing things to suit the new normal. When you allow for the fluid evolution of your plans and processes you can respond more easily to what's happening personally, with your family, team members, and whatever is going on in the market.

LIVING WITH S.A.S.S. IS YOU AS THE BEST VERSION OF YOU

The change we bring to the world by being the best version of ourselves and focusing on what's most important moves everyone forward. Know that our world needs connection and love, compassion and understanding, as much we need doing and achieving by women who value those things. The subsequent chapters will take you deeper into each of the pillars so you can take a closer look at how these concepts are relevant for you. Congratulations on getting started on your new adventure of living with S.A.S.S.

REFLECT:

On a scale from 0–10 with 10 being *your* ideal, how would you rate how **SIMPLE** things are in your life and work? Where would you like to be?

CURRENT RATING: DESIRED RATING:

What would it take to reach your desired rating (besides a miracle)?

On a scale from 0–10 with 10 being *your* ideal, how would you rate how **ALIGNED** you are in your life and work?

CURRENT RATING: DESIRED RATING:

What would it take to reach your desired rating (besides a miracle)?

On a scale from 0–10 with 10 being *your* ideal, how would you rate how **SUSTAINABLE** your life and work are for you? Where would you like to be?

CURRENT RATING: **DESIRED RATING:**

What would it take to reach your desired rating (besides a miracle)?

On a scale from 0–10 with 10 being *your* ideal, how would you rate how **SYSTEMIZED** you are in your life and work? Where would you like to be?

CURRENT RATING: **DESIRED RATING:**

What would it take to reach your desired rating (besides a miracle)?

In what ways would living with S.A.S.S. bring value to your life?

IMPLEMENT:

What is one step you're committed to taking this week to bring your life and work more into alignment with the S.A.S.S. philosophy?

YOU HAVE A CHOICE:
CONTINUE TO LIVE THE WAY YOU HAVE, *OR*
UPLEVEL YOUR LIFE & RESULTS WITH S.A.S.S.

WHICH DO YOU PICK?

THE S.A.S.S. SYSTEM:

<u>S</u>IMPLE

CHAPTER FOUR:

SIMPLICITY WINS

THERE WAS A TIME IN MY LIFE THAT WAS ANYTHING BUT SIMple. I lived in a sprawling four-bedroom house. Every bedroom had space to do cartwheels around a king bed. Every closet was full. Clutter was everywhere. The garage was so full of things a car couldn't be parked in either spot for as long as I lived there.

I ran two businesses and supported my partner with marketing a third. When someone asked me what I did, I never knew what to say. Did I tell them I was a graphic designer? A web developer? An energy healer? A stress and anxiety relief facilitator?

I wanted to be free of everything but I didn't know how. Even going through a single closet felt heavy and overwhelming. Looking in the garage was just evidence of the past. Apart from the fact that I didn't have kids, every other part of my life felt complicated.

I worried about there never being enough. I had to collect things and stuff out of a need to feel safe. I spent money hand over fist because I needed to *have it all* and once I bought something new there was always something more to have. It never ended.

Over time I steadily began letting go. I lived in progressively smaller places with less and less storage space. I wrapped up the old businesses I didn't like and currently work solely with high achieving women. And by simplifying, now that I have less, I feel as though I have more—more time, more energy, and more enjoyment.

The idea of having much more stuff and responsibilities feels overly burdensome: both wasteful and distracting. I now recognize I was trying to cover up for some of the unresolved wounds I had been carrying from my family. I had learned that that's what adults do—they get stuff, and they do many things. Somehow both were measures of my achievement.

* * *

Finding Balance

Now admittedly, I still like things. I've considered becoming a digital nomad and what it would take to live with everything I owned in carry-on baggage. That feels like a stretch and I have no interest currently in taking things to that extreme.

There is a balance for sure. And what I've found is that the simpler my life gets, the more I focus on doing things in the least complicated way possible, the more I am able to be free to be me. With simplicity I let myself shine through in my personal and professional relationships.

What I've noticed is that when I choose the complicated path all that happens is that I wind up sick and tired and overwhelmed and stagnant. Choices that can take me there include when I try to be too much to too many people all at once, when I create unnecessary processes, and when I collect too many things and too much clutter.

We were designed for simplicity in some ways. Our senses are only useful to us in the present moment and this was how we were meant to experience reality. And yet, we layer reality on top of reality on top of reality. This creates confusion and chaos where there had previously been none.

* * *

Discovering Sacred Simplicity

When I was seventeen, I took a canoeing trip up to Saskatchewan, Canada, with six other women. We paddled over 400 miles in 30 days. It was on this trip that I realized how little I actually needed in order to live a satisfying life: food, shelter, dry clothes, and some friends to laugh and cry with as we shared the adventures.

I remember I was sitting out by a river where we had camped late one afternoon. The rush of the water pouring by me filled my ears. No other music was needed. I was writing in my journal and reflecting on how where I was in that moment was perfection. I could envision myself staying in that place forever and being completely satisfied—perhaps a modern day Henry David Thoreau.

And yet, there was this other part of me that knew that my purpose was not to check out, and staying in this place and unplugging would be doing that. Instead, I needed to bring more of the sacred simplicity and what I had learned on this trip back to the regular world. It was of use to no one for me to unplug and separate.

Forgetting What I Knew

Even with that wisdom and awareness at seventeen, it didn't keep me from getting sucked into an addiction with mass consumerism. I left that place of sacred simplicity in nature and when I returned to the modern world I forgot what I knew.

I grew up and got caught up in my career. I bought a house, several of them actually, and filled them with tons of stuff. It took me a long time to step out of this programming.

My parents had a lot of stuff. So what I had learned was that it was normal to live in a big house with all the closets filled with things. That's what I was working toward. It's normal to recreate exactly what you know.

I had forgotten what I had learned at seventeen: that stuff didn't matter. People and experiences did. That doing things in a simple way meant more space to appreciate everything.

What I didn't realize was that collecting things kept me safe distracting myself, kept me fulfilling the status quo as defined by giant corporations, and inadvertently kept me from having what I really wanted in my life. What I wanted was greater connection, greater community, and greater awareness of myself.

It took me a long time to shift from a reality of MORE, MORE, MORE—taking everything for granted, and creating endless complexity through my personal and professional choices. Now I value every item for its unique usefulness, I streamline where it adds value, and I have gratitude for everything—even those thirty pairs of underwear that I keep because then I don't have to do laundry often.

At one time I thought moving into a big girl home with a beautiful view of the mountains and water would make me happy. I quickly learned that this was not the case. That it didn't matter where I lived or how much money I made, that the only way to achieve happiness was to be it, not buy it.

* * *

SIMPLIFYING HOME & WORK

I eventually moved from that giant house into progressively smaller homes. Each stage I downsized. And then downsized again. And then downsized again. Things got simpler and simpler. I don't even remember what I sold off in those garage sales anymore. All I know is that I don't miss any of it.

My professional world shifted too. I went from having my finger in three different pies to one. Simple wins on all fronts personally and professionally. No more wondering what I say when someone asks me what I do. My energy all flows in a singular direction. Mentoring high achieving women is the entire focus of what I do now.

* * *

SIMPLICITY WITH A FAMILY

Some people seem to think that simplicity only works if you don't have a family—that what I've done has been possible because I don't have kids.

Though what I know to be true is that simplicity becomes even more important when you have a family. Keeping things simple helps you focus on what's most important. It turns out that most people don't arrive at simplicity without a lot of turmoil. And that turmoil becomes a catalyst for changing the way they operate.

Jewels Muller is good example of this. She's the founder of ChicksConnect, a community of mastermind groups for women business owners. She now has women leading seventy-four groups across the United States and in the last six years has had about a thousand members between them.

And though she could choose to live anywhere, the lifestyle that suits her best is to live a simple life with her husband and two children on the road in a three hundred square foot motor home. These days she says, "I feel blessed and lucky to be living the way I'm meant to be living." But getting there nearly cost her sanity and her marriage.

* * *

ARRIVING AT SIMPLICITY THE HARD WAY

At one time Jewels and her husband owned several homes and businesses in Bend, Oregon. They appeared successful on the outside, but underneath she was a highly stressed, over-scheduled, high achieving super-doer.

And then in 2007 her husband made a mistake and underbid a lighting retrofit project by five months and several hundred thousand dollars. The client insisted he honor his original bid.

Dealing with the ramifications of this caused their world to come crashing down. To cover their employee wages while the company completed the project, Jewels and her husband double-mortgaged their homes thinking that more money would come. It didn't.

"We joke that we were the first to the downfall of the economy in 2008. We lost everything," Jewels reflected.

This made her already stressful life even more complicated. To scrape by, she did anything she could. She worked as a coach, sold SendOutCards, and did custom closets and professional organizing in multi-million dollar homes. She was embarrassed to be a forty-year-old living with two kids in what she considered to be a crummy apartment.

Recovering from this error put her marriage through the wringer. Under this extreme financial strain Jewels became angry, resentful, lonely, and exhausted. Functionally she was a single mom to her twins while her husband worked out of town to complete this money pit of a project. She thought regularly about divorce.

She eventually intuited the idea for ChicksConnect simply as a way to grow her other businesses. A year later her vision had become to develop a worldwide community. She was intuitively guided that it was time to "hit the road and meet the women face to face."

While her husband was supportive of the idea, she and her family were still struggling financially at the time. ChicksConnect had less than one hundred members from which she netted about three hundred dollars a month. Her husband was having difficulty getting work.

Life as she knew it was miserable. She would joke about her circumstances, asking friends, "When can I schedule my mental breakdown?" She didn't think she could stop for a moment or what little she had left would fall apart too.

It was time to do something different, so acting on pure faith and a plan to give ChicksConnect everything she had, she and her family took the leap and got rid of everything and hit the road in a motor home.

* * *

Enjoying the Benefits of Simplicity

The theme of simplicity at the core of everything helped her keep her sanity. In three hundred square feet shared by four people there isn't room for anything non-essential. "If you love it and use it then keep it. But if you don't love it and use it then lose it," she explained, "Give it to someone who will honor and cherish it."

Professionally, she's devoted 100% of her focus to ChicksConnect. When she went mobile she dropped her custom closet sales and professional organizing business. This helped her make fast progress with ChicksConnect when she otherwise would've been spread too thin. And by being mobile she had the freedom to travel to many more communities while still maintaining her commitments to her family.

Plus, "Had I stayed local I would've busied myself with micromanaging the local chapters." Instead, she empowered leaders to use her structure and to create the chapters in the ways that they wanted. By keeping things simple she made it possible to build systems that would run without her intervention. Simplicity made freedom much easier.

* * *

How Life Has Changed

Jewels used to put in twelve-hour days as someone self-described as "hardwired to work." Now she sees her kids all the time and can go be with her parents when they are sick. She doesn't overconsume anymore and is much more comfortable within her financial commitments.

She takes time to do yoga, meditation, and connect with people over coffee, or even to do nothing occasionally. These were activities she didn't even see as valuable before. She's no longer tired because self-care and rest are now built into the routine.

And she has time to nurture and enjoy relationships that matter because she isn't overcommitted and running from one thing to the next on her calendar. Her relationship with her husband is solid again and he's been her biggest cheerleader. She is grateful and appreciative of everything in her life.

* * *

WE EACH HAVE OUR OWN IDEAL VERSION OF SIMPLE

Focusing on simplicity takes you to the core of what matters to you and eliminates everything else. Yet each woman has her own perfect definition of what simple looks like. There is no hard rule about narrowing your wardrobe to twenty pieces or living with your entire family in three hundred square feet.

Personally, I still am far off from being a digital nomad who only owns what fits in two small carry-ons. I wouldn't want to live with my family in a motor home. As an introvert who needs time alone I'd go crazy.

Though when I challenged myself the other day with a game—if I had to edit my shoes down to only three pairs, which would I keep? There wasn't any thought, my answer was instantaneous and easy. This was a surprise even to me: one pair of Tevas sandals, one pair of leather ankle high boots for work, one pair of black leather Keens. When you know what matters to you and what your needs are, simplicity is the winning solution that becomes part of your DNA.

* * *

WHERE TO START WITH SIMPLIFYING

1. Start small. A junk drawer is a perfect place to begin streamlining. Why there? Jewels explains, "The practice of organization is a little mindless. And doing that will help free you up to think about how you can make other changes in your personal [life] and work."

2. When you're finished, don't forget to celebrate. Jewels suggests that celebrating, "Anchors the habit of taking steps toward what you want instead of what you don't want." This supports your natural motivation to continue.

REFLECT:

What have you done a good job of keeping simple in your life?

Where in your life or work have you made things more complicated than would be helpful?

What is one thing you could simplify personally or professionally that would reduce your stress, strain, or energy drain?

How would doing this positively impact your life?

IMPLEMENT:

What one step towards simplifying will you commit to doing this week?

Want more time,
energy, or money?

Simplicity is efficiency.

CHAPTER FIVE:

CHOOSE QUALITY OVER QUANTITY

"Here, can you open these?"

My nephew handed me two more plastic balls filled with gold colored plastic necklaces. They had emblems of dollar signs and thumbs up on them.

I sighed. I'd already opened at least five of these already. He had spent all his quarters but still had another crisp five dollar bill in his hand. And he couldn't help but spend that too. He eagerly skipped over to the cashier to exchange it for more quarters to feed the machines so he could get more plastic balls with golden necklaces made in China inside.

There was no game to play, no experience beyond the insertion of the coins into the slots and the turning of the crank. The only enjoyment was in the immediate gratification of that ball rolling out into his hand—the getting. And not just once or twice, but rather, getting more, and more, and more.

When the money he had finally run out, he left the mini golf place victorious, wearing those golden plastic necklaces with as much pride as an Olympian wears a medal, all twenty of them around his neck at once.

And when he arrived home, in an instant he was off to something else and those necklaces were discarded on the kitchen table and have never been played with again.

* * *

When is Enough, Enough?

I think about this experience quite often. Mainly because of how stressful it was to witness someone in a manic state of wanting more, more, more and not being able to satiate themselves.

And yet, this isn't that unusual of an experience. We live in a society that values more, more, more. We don't need one pair of shoes, we need fifty. We don't need one college degree, how about two? Once we make $50,000, why not $100,000, why not $350,000?

Exactly when is enough, enough? Often times instead of appreciating and celebrating what we have and where we are, we just roll into the next "more" thing whether or not it makes any sense or is aligned for us. This idea that wherever we are or what we have is not enough is pervasive, particularly amongst achievers.

And like my nephew, it's easy to get caught up in the fervor of getting and achieving, especially when we don't slow down. And it's when we don't slow down that it's easy to forget the original purpose behind getting a car or a house or achieving an income level or getting a promotion. I recognize this in myself because I can be rather compulsive too.

MY OWN COMPULSION

There are two things I really enjoy (well more than that, but two I'm going to tell you about right now). One, I really like Target®, it's my favorite chain store. And two, I like a great deal. Combine the two together = paradise.

Awhile back, Target® used to put all their clearance on the end caps facing the exterior aisle that goes around the whole store. Sometimes they do this now, but now most of the stuff that would've been highly discounted now finds itself donated to Goodwill® instead.

But prior to this, my partner and I used to go to the store purposefully to walk and shop the clearance along that outer aisle. We'd make a date out of it, get our red shopping cart and sit our $1 bag of popcorn and an ICEE® in the cart seat like a baby. We'd walk and eat popcorn and slurp our sugary drink and find great deals on stuff we didn't need.

The trouble was I'd go home with a bag of stuff I'd bought that would then sit unopened still in the shopping bag in the middle of my living room. At the time I had housemates so I'm not sure what they thought of that, it couldn't have been good. Especially because the pile of things in bags I didn't need got bigger and bigger and bigger. I got the instant gratification out of finding a great deal, though beyond that it was just a wasted investment that created clutter and distraction for more than just me.

On the upside I will say I have been putting up ten cent wall hooks in each of the last six homes I've lived in. So maybe some part of it was useful after all—but I had to haul them around for many years too!

The Infatuation with Being Busy

Shopping and consumerism isn't the only area in our lives where MORE can get the better of us though. It shows up in other areas too. It's considered normal, even desirable culturally, to be busy all the time.

In fact it's one of the most common phrases I hear from people when I ask them how they are. "Oh, I'm good, I'm busy!" I consider this part of our infatuation with MORE.

Running from one thing to the next somehow means we are important, contributing, growing, or valuable. So we overschedule our kids, we overschedule ourselves, and then we all get stressed, cranky, tired, and burned out.

The only solution to any of this is to slow down. To slow down and let it be okay to focus on quality over quantity. To slow down and then remember why we're doing what we're doing and why we're investing in what we're investing in. To slow down and be fully present.

Only when we do this can we decide if something is really supporting us at all. And if we're winding up cranky and exhausted at the end of the day, then a choice or collection of choices is probably not aligned for us.

* * *

Contribution & a Full Human Experience

In my world, being successful is as much about living a life of contribution as it is about having a full human experience while doing that. Overdoing or overhaving doesn't support the balance of either concept.

Being mindful of quantity is important because having MORE often requires additional energy to maintain. This can increase our stress load unless we offset any increased required energy or responsibility with greater support.

A bigger house is more to clean and more things that may need repairs. The more children, friends, or staff members we have, the more energy is required to nurture those relationships. A larger wardrobe requires making more decisions when getting dressed. More plants in the garden then require fertilization, weeding, and watering. Having more inventory could mean more opportunity for sales. It also could mean greater opportunity for losses and waste.

So when you desire or invite the MORE into your life, the key is to be mindful of the reason you're doing it. Keeping things simple and focusing on quality and impact creates the opportunity to invest time, energy, and resources into what matters most for you.

And even better, when we make aligned choices that reflect valuing quality over quantity, we also enable ourselves to step out of that feeling of never being enough. How? We stop subconsciously trying to prove our enoughness by having more for the sake of more, of achieving more for the sake of achieving more, of doing more for the sake of doing more.

REFLECT:

Where are you already great at living out the concept that LESS is MORE in your life?

Where are you overconsuming (or overscheduling)?

Where would it be helpful for you to shift your focus to valuing and appreciating quality over quantity?

How would focusing on quality over quantity decrease your stress level or add to your enjoyment or effectiveness?

And how would that benefit others?

IMPLEMENT:

And what is one thing you're committed to doing differently to shift your focus from quantity to quality this week?

.

Would what you desire add value
& improve the quality of your
life or work?

Or, is it another golden plastic
necklace to string around your neck?

CHAPTER SIX:

STREAMLINE YOUR FOCUS

Eggs. I woke up with a singular thought this morning. I needed to go to the store and get some eggs so I could have breakfast. I hadn't been doing a very good job of feeding myself and it would be helpful for this to be a higher priority. All my brain power needed to be firing on all cylinders today.

I woke up. I knew exactly what I needed to do. And by the time my feet hit the floor it had already gone sideways. It wasn't until noon that I was actually eating eggs.

Up until that point, I had answered email, scheduled an interview, booked someone to join me on a mastermind call, and worked on negotiating some financing issues. Everything except get eggs or eat them.

I had been productive. And I still hadn't done things in my best order of priority: take care of *me* first. That meant my focus was off and too broad today.

It can be really easy to get off track from our highest priorities even when we know what those are. It doesn't matter whether that is a focus on our health or a focus on professional goals like launching a new project or hitting a particular revenue goal. There are always a bizillion shiny objects and distractions.

It is so easy to spread ourselves too thin doing too many things at once. And if we don't keep focused intently on the few things that matter most it means that those high priorities don't happen.

Want to know how easy it is to get off track? Just look at me. I know this stuff. I teach this stuff. And it still happens to me sometimes. I woke up this morning knowing exactly where I needed to start and I still didn't do it. I had one thought one minute, and the next minute I was onto something else.

* * *

What Did I Do That Didn't Work?

I didn't get focused with my usual routine. I didn't start with my highest priorities: feeding myself, beautifying my space, walking outside, and having some deep inner listening. That process works well for me.

Instead, I sat down at the computer and started working rather than dealing with the single issue I had in mind when I woke up: eggs. I got into doing and got lost.

Have you ever had in mind a task, even something so simple as having breakfast or returning a call to a key contact, and you start your day with every intention of doing that thing. But before you turn around you're totally involved with something else and the end of the day rolls around and that task at top of your list never happened?

Relentless Commitment & Focus

In a world with so many distractions, achievement in any area whether it's health, relationships, finances, or work requires one thing: relentless commitment and focus.

If our focus gets too broad, if we let ourselves get distracted by too many projects, people, and activities, we lose. Plain and simple.

The most common place my clients often notice that they get lost is in marketing activities. They're trying to pursue and manage too many initiatives all at once because some guru somewhere said this thing or that thing was essential to their business. Unless you have a big team, it's not possible to focus on growing your social media engagement on Twitter, Facebook, LinkedIn, Pinterest, and Instagram, and growing your email list, starting a podcast, increasing client refer- rals, improving client retention, and doing ad campaigns all at once.

And even if you have a big team, focusing in all these areas at once can be distracting and dilute focus and results for your team as well. If you tried to do all of these yourself you would typically feel like a chicken running around without a head.

This is an example of how there can be so many balls in the air that even the organized and well-intentioned will drop some. It can happen in any area of life.

When you're running in so many different directions it's overwhelming, it's confusing, it's frustrating, sometimes dis- appointing, and often stressful. And when we approach any aspect of life or work this way, it delays and sometimes dimin- ishes our results.

Instead, as often as possible, as relentlessly as possible, fo- cus on one thing at a time. If you want to achieve more, know that multi-tasking takes you off track. Every time you change activities or shift your focus you lose time. So keep your focus narrow and singular.

* * *

Focus = Buckets of Attention, Time, & Energy

I consider focus itself to be the specific bucket where I place my attention, time, and energy. There might singular or multiple tangible, measurable goals related to and within a focus.

But goals themselves never get achieved without the nurturing close container of focus. And when focus is too big and broad or shifts between too many different buckets, the goals get lost. Achievement without tight focus is limited.

My biggest bucket, my focus for the year is more of a theme. I've found it's helpful to streamline my focus in my life so that I have particular personal and professional themes where I invest my energy and attention within a calendar year. Then my strategy is to align the majority of my specific goals and activities within the focus of those themes or buckets.

In 2016, I had one focus, build relationships and get rooted in Minneapolis where I had just moved after getting divorced after eighteen years with my partner. Everything else personally and professionally took a back seat to that.

On a day-to-day basis, my goals and activities were aligned with that focus. I dated. I had great sex. I made friends and met amazing people. I went to social gatherings. I went camping and paddled the local lakes. I danced. I chanted and meditated. I built my social and professional network.

I grieved what had ended and explored and recovered parts of myself. I took personal development trainings. I spent more time with my parents and sister than I had in the previous 20 years combined.

In 2017, my focus was on two things. Professionally: creating reliable, consistent, predictable contribution and cash flow through my business. My impact and monthly income had been all over the map and neither was satisfying or sustainable long term.

All my activities were focused around that. So over the year I streamlined my service offerings and refined my target market and messaging to clearly communicate the results of working with me. And I got more visible—much more visible. This book is a part of that.

My primary marketing and focus of my contribution became speaking gigs, interviews, and podcasts that are now on the calendar up to a year in advance. This consistently got me in front of women who want to achieve bigger goals more enjoyably without feeling drained or burned out.

This naturally led to more opportunities to connect directly with ideal clients, helped inspire and move many others forward with the message, and created more consistent cash flow in my business.

Personally: my focus for the year was food. Specifically, eating more regularly and healthfully, thus the eggs registering so prominently in my consciousness this morning.

I know, eating is probably a simple thing for most people, for me it's been a struggle. My pattern has been that when I have gotten busy I have forgotten to eat.

The reason why this was such a priority is because in 2016 my immune system was really low. I had viruses six times in the year and most other years this only happened once or twice. It felt like I was getting sick every time I turned around and it wasn't something I wanted to continue.

I knew the solution was more consistency with food since remembering to eat was never my strength. Living alone without someone sharing meal prep hadn't helped things. I'd consistently get sick after a week or so of missing meals regularly and not eating well.

At the beginning of 2017 I started cooking for myself again versus relying on prepackaged convenience foods. I figured out a system that had me making meals once a week that I could freeze and heat up easily through the week. I was eating more consistently which was helpful.

Over the summer I progressed to eating the Whole30® program. For six weeks I ate no processed food, grains, added sugars, dairy, or legumes. Just simple meals with protein and veggies and some fruit. I'd done this before and already knew it was what my body liked.

That's was great and I still mostly eat that way. Meal prep became more enjoyable even though this way of eating is more work because my new partner and I started doing at least half of the dinners together. Food became fun.

But because most of these fresh foods don't freeze and reheat well, I hadn't figured out the routine about making ready-to-go frozen food. So I started falling into the old pattern again of getting overwhelmed by the idea of meal prep, getting busy, and then forgetting to eat. Even making eggs can seem like an inconvenience. And this was exactly where I landed again today.

* * *

WHAT TO DO WHEN WE SCREW UP?

Time to streamline my focus again and recommit. Just like any commitment, it matters more that we do something consistently rather than that we do it perfectly.

More days than not I've been getting my focus on food right. I'm certainly doing better overall than last year. Today I didn't do well. It's okay.

The reality is that no matter how good we are at staying focused on our highest priorities, some days we fall off the wagon just like I did today. It's not a travesty.

I'm a recovering perfectionist, so I've had a habit of beating myself up over the years for not being perfect, for not doing things as well as I could've. I've realized that this process doesn't help me make new choices and do better, it just puts my focus on negative feelings about myself which inevitably keeps perpetuating the old behavior I don't want.

The truth is, I mess up. I mess up a ton. And I'm okay with being perfectly gorgeously, beautifully imperfect. (Most days!) Failure is feedback.

And recognizing I wasn't staying focused on my highest commitment is simply an opportunity to notice what could use some adjustment so I can choose differently tomorrow. Or when it comes to dinner which I'm due for right now. Fish tacos anyone?

✳ ✳ ✳

5 Tips for Streamlining Your Focus on a Daily Basis

1. Do not start your day with email. Email has other people's priorities in it, not yours. Instead, start your day with a high priority project that will move you forward. You'll get that one thing done and immediately feel like you're off to a good start for the day. Do this for a whole year and imagine how much more you'll accomplish! Catch up with your email after you've spend sixty to ninety minutes on that priority project.

2. Use a To-Do List as a "brain dump" rather than your task list. This list is a way to empty your mind so you can focus, not determine your projects for the

day. Jot down anything on the list that you're thinking about or don't want to forget. Whatever's rat-
tling around in your brain, just put it on the page.
   Then set the list aside to focus on your one or two
highest priority projects you've already determined. Or
alternatively, activities that are directly revenue generating (if it's work). If while you're working your mind
distracts you with something other than the activity
you're working on, pull out the list, add your thoughts
to the list, and then set it aside again. Let anything on
the list that isn't both important and urgent go.

3. Do something you're excited about working on everyday. Motivation is naturally fueled by excitement. It's
   easier to get stuff done. If your whole schedule doesn't
   have anything you're excited about then it will be easy
   to get burned out and harder to stay focused.

4. Go for a walk. If your mind is jumping all around it's
   time to take a break and do something physical. Take
   a short walk even if it's just around the block and be
   present with appreciating your surroundings, noticing
   what you see, smell, hear, and even touch. When you
   come back you'll be able to start again and see things
   with fresh eyes.

5. Stack like activities together. Different activities have
   different energies and switching between a bunch
   of varied tasks is counter productive. So put like activities together when possible. For example, writing and lead generation activities I usually do on
   Marketing Mondays. I see clients Tuesdays through
   Thursdays. On Financial Fridays I do all financial
   activities together.

REFLECT:

What is your top professional focus right now for the next 3–12 months?

How are you willing to adjust your goals, schedule, or activities so that this gets the majority of your attention and energy?

What is your top personal focus right now for the next 3–12 months?

How do you choose to adjust your goals, schedule, or activities so that this gets top billing on your priority list?

IMPLEMENT:

What are you ready to let go of as you streamline your focus to these two buckets so you increase your impact and reduce your stress?

What one step are you committed to completing this week that moves you in this direction?

When you dilute your focus
you delay & diminish your results.

THE S.A.S.S. SYSTEM:

ALIGNED (TO YOU)

CHAPTER SEVEN:

FOLLOW YOUR HEART
& INTUITION

ONE MORNING RECENTLY I WAS STRATEGIZING WITH A CONsultant about a promo on a launch I was doing.

"So what do you think, do you want to make this offer to everyone or just to part of this one special group?" she asked.

My head went off in a spin. "Oh YES, offer it to everyone—if it turns out they don't want it, it's no big deal, they'll just opt out of my email list," my mind instantly rattled.

My heart, my body, my intuition had an entirely different answer: a very clear NO. Keep it simple. Only make the promotional offer to the special group, not everyone. As I scanned my attention up and down my body, everything felt smooth and calm, no tension that would indicate I was afraid and needed to probe further.

And without any other further consideration, the decision was made. Only make the offer to the smaller group, not my entire list.

* * *

DECISIONS BY INTUITION

Following my heart and using my intuition has become an integral part of my world. I use it to make every kind of decision in life and business. This includes everything from which produce to buy at the grocery store to deciding what marketing strategies to implement. (Yes, I actually ask the apples which ones will support me on the path I'm on and pick the ones that draw my attention.) And of course, I use my intuition to guide the flow of sessions with clients.

Following your heart and using your intuition is helpful anytime, and especially so if you're struggling with feeling drained and burned out. Both are symptoms of saying YES to too many things that are not aligned for you. Making aligned choices is about welcoming things into your life and work that fit for you on all levels: mind, body, and spirit.

If you're feeling drained and burned out it's because you've been saying YES to things your mind tells you that you *should* do, not because what you're doing is actually a fit for you. Following your heart and intuition instead can turn this around.

Some people know their intuition as their gut instinct or inner wisdom. It gives you access to information that exists unseen all around us on channels other than the mental level.

It can be that some information comes through the mind itself, though most people have difficulty discerning this from their own clutter of thought patterns. This is why it's easier to get started by focusing on listening to what the body is doing as I did when deciding about my promotional strategy.

Opening to the flow of intuition isn't easy when we're set up to fail at it. In western culture we were socialized to believe that listening to our gut instinct, our inner knowing that goes beyond what we can rationalize is…insane. Nobody wants to be considered crazy including me.

Many believe that logic is the only way to make good decisions. And it is regularly reinforced that listening to our body, our hearts, our feelings, our inner wisdom is both foolish and stupid. That's why a lot of people don't do it.

So listening and following your heart and intuition is by definition, a revolutionary act. It goes against everything our culture tells us is real. And yet, those things are very much real and designed to support us in creating more enjoyable human experiences. All other things being equal, logic only gets you so far.

* * *

INTUITION IN MY WORKFLOW

When I go into a client session, I consider my job to be to show up and follow directions. I do not do my work with my mind; I listen intuitively to which questions my guides and spiritual team encourage, sometimes emphatically prod me to ask.

Who are my guides and spiritual team? Well they are many beings on the other side not currently embodied that help me. Typically they speak to me in one voice though that voice represents a very large advisory team. They have permission only to deliver what is in my highest and best good and the highest and best good of all those involved.

When I work with clients, I lean into these guides to run my sessions. I follow willingly down seemingly random rabbit holes if my mind were to judge them. But by following these leads, it turns out to efficiently solve whatever issue the client has in a completely nonlinear way.

For example, I had a client who opened our session with an intention to resolve something related to her professional career where she was struggling. As our conversation continued she made a seemingly unrelated offhand comment about her brother.

I was guided to ask her a question about that comment which eventually led to an intense discovery about how he contributed to her experience of sexual abuse even though he was not directly involved.

She reflected on the limiting beliefs related to the trauma that were affecting her now. Together, we shifted her feeling about her experience of her relationship with her brother. And then we installed some more helpful beliefs which clearly led to the resolution of the issue in her work.

My mind would never have taken me down that road. Following my intuition did. Turns out, my mind never knows the solution to much. My mind is really good at 2+2=4, 4+4=8. Computations and planning certainly has its place. Yet the mind does not have the range of access to unseen information in the way that my heart and intuition do.

* * *

SCIENCE SUPPORTING INTUITION

There's actually science supporting the idea that our heart knows things faster than our brain. Researchers at HeartMath have done studies where a participant was hooked up to a bunch of instruments that measured various aspects of the body's responsiveness. They were then shown random images on the computer as chosen by the computer itself. Not even the researcher knew which ones would be selected.

Some of these images were calming: beautiful scenery and flowers, puppies, and kitties. And some of the images were shocking and emotionally evocative: crime scene photos and horror shots.

As the participants were shown the photos, the researchers measured the person's physiological responses to the images. Here's what they found: the heart responded to the image whether calming or stressful *faster* than the brain.

In fact, the heart responded appropriately to the images in more than half of the participants *before* the image had even been randomly chosen by the computer. That meant that their body responded intuitively to the situation without them even consciously knowing what was going to happen next.

Bodies are smart in ways we have historically not acknowledged. Just because you can't see something or it can't be quantified doesn't mean it isn't there. There are many unseen parameters when making decisions. And one cannot always predict with the mind when something unanticipated will happen. But when you tap into the wisdom of your body, the wisdom of your intuition, not only can you often anticipate the unexpected, by listening and following this information you can make choices that are more aligned for you.

* * *

FOLLOWING INTUITIVE NUDGES LEADS TO MORE GRACE & EASE

Quite a few years back I was planning a family vacation with my then partner and in-laws. This is one of my favorite things to do. I love researching about travel, figuring out where to go, what to do, and how to get the best deal on the adventure I have in mind.

Those who have traveled with me know that they just need to come along and they will have a good time, eat great food, and have plenty of interesting choices of things to do each day that are mostly determined by how everyone feels.

This one particular year Thailand was looking very fun. I wanted to go to Bangkok and Chiang Mai and somewhere by the beach. I started researching all the options. I found this great deal for an all-inclusive tour with airfare. I told everyone in the group about it—they were very excited too. So we decided to book.

For some reason when I started to book us, I couldn't find any reasonably priced airfare included in the package from where I lived at the time. It all looked really good on paper. My in-laws who were coming from Los Angeles could get the deal just fine. But there was no way to come up with airfare from Portland, Oregon that was anywhere close to the original price that had been offered for our departure airport.

I didn't want to spend double the money. That wasn't my style—I wanted a deal. And as it stood, booking this vacation felt difficult, heavy, and complicated.

So after some discussion with my partner, we decided we weren't going to go. As much as it seemed like this was the trip we wanted, intuitively we knew not to force something that wasn't happening easily.

My in-laws on the other hand were thrilled I had found them a fabulous cheap holiday and *did* go on the trip. While they were there, huge tsunamis hit the coast of Thailand and thousands died and were injured. (Fortunately my in-laws were inland at the time of the tour so were safe.)

When this happened, it made complete sense to me why I had difficulty booking the trip and why when it came to following through paying more for the flights it didn't feel comfortable at all to do so. My heart felt heavy and forcing something that didn't flow easily didn't feel like honoring the intuitive nudge that had been given.

Now I'm a highly sensitive, empathic person and being in a place so close to where so many people transitioned to the other side all at once would not be the most graceful idea for me. I would empathically be experiencing the deep grieving of all the people left behind and encountering plenty of lost souls. This would have been overwhelming.

My mind said go to Thailand. My heart said this is not the trip for you at this time. Fortunately my heart won out in this case.

Many times the evidence of what happens when we follow our intuition and heart is not as resoundingly clear as this— because we don't get to see what happens if we had chosen the alternative. But because I've had so much experience and feedback about what happens when I do follow, I now generally trust the feedback my body gives me and that I get intuitively from my guides.

* * *

DO MISTAKES HAPPEN WHEN MAKING CHOICES THIS WAY?

Of course. Certainly there would be things I would do-over if I could occasionally. For one, buying that house at the top of the housing bubble would've been a great one to skip.

But what I learned through that experience was priceless. So this "misstep" was absolutely a gift for me even though I wouldn't have picked it with my mind. I still would love to have that money I lost back in my bank account—while at the same time I wouldn't trade it for the wisdom I received though the experience.

At this point, my intuition is highly tuned. I've had plenty of time to test what works for me and what doesn't and get feedback from the results I experience. Without question, I get better results overall from listening to my intuition than my mind—and because I make aligned decisions for me I stay happier and healthier too.

* * *

Intuitive Skills Everyone Needs

While I believe it is possible that with practice everyone can hear their guides clearly and have intuitive visions, most people don't start there. And this level of information isn't even necessary to navigate by intuition on a day-to-day basis.

As I discuss in detail in my programs, the skills I believe everyone needs are to be able to listen to your heart and intuition so that when you are offered an opportunity you get a clear answer of whether something is a YES for you or a NO.

Women get stuck in indecision or make choices that aren't aligned for them that lead to stress, mess, and burn out when they don't have clear processes to determine whether something is a fit for them or not. If you can decide easily whether something is a YES or a NO for you by listening to your body and inner wisdom you have exactly what you need to navigate by intuition.

* * *

Three Steps to Begin Tapping into Your Body's Wisdom

Step 1: Bring a simple yes or no question to mind.

Step 2: Take a few deep breaths and bring your attention to the area of your body where you would like more information. (Start with your heart in the center of your chest, then your gut.) Ask the question again.

Step 3: Notice whatever you notice. How does it FEEL? (Not what do you think about it, that will take you right back to your mind.) Does it feel open? Light? Exciting? Those are usually indicators of YES. Does it feel tight? Dark? Heavy? Those are usually indicators of NO or that it's scary and needs some further investigation.

Pay attention to what shows up for you. Everyone's indicators are different and do not need to follow any common pattern across the board. One of my clients sees a vision of a big green swirling that means something is a YES for her. Your YES or NO might be unique to you also. Take notes and follow the patterns.

* * *

HANDLING DOUBT

Doubt is real and shows up even for me. Every week I have client sessions where I'm being shown by my intuitive helpers to do something and my response is, "You want me to do what???"

It's not about avoiding doubt, it's about developing so much trust in yourself that you're willing to walk through the fire of doubt knowing you won't get burned. And to do this requires remembering that being imperfect IS perfect and letting go of attachment to the outcome.

When I get intuitive messages in client sessions that seem crazy, I resist sharing for a bit and then eventually surrender to the idea when my helpers keep pestering me. I don't want to look stupid in front of my clients and sometimes whatever my guides ask me to do seems ridiculous.

One time they told me to ask my client to pretend as though she had a big pile of spaghetti on her head and to take her hands and imagine she was pulling each individual noodle out of the pile away from her head. This sounded crazy. But they wouldn't give up so finally I surrendered to the idea of requesting my client to play along.

So I asked her, "I have this wacky idea that I can't get out of my head. I'm not sure exactly where it will go, would you be open to playing a little game with me and see?"

Without fail in a scenario like this, something brilliant happens. In this case, after pulling away the strands of spaghetti, the client reported the headache that she hadn't even told me about was gone.

Doubt stems from the idea that certain outcomes or experiences are better than others and we want to experience whatever our mind judges to be good or right or pleasurable. We don't want to make a mistake and create a *bad* or *unpleasurable* outcome.

In reality, all options are neither good or bad. They each come with consequences or results. Some results are more consciously pleasurable than others. However, often the most challenging things we experience tend to be the most helpful for us long term as we learn and grow.

It is our mind that assigns judgments liberally. When in reality, an action or experience is not good or bad based on the nature of the act itself. All acts and experiences are inherently neutral. It is our belief systems and survival mechanisms that tell us that they aren't.

One of the keys to moving through doubt and taking action anyway is shifting out of the mindset that there are right and wrong choices—that there are good or bad outcomes. We worry that we will get it wrong, look silly, stupid, or unprofessional (which most of us believe subconsciously makes us unlovable). All of those are judgments assigned by our mind out of fear based on whatever we believe.

Mantras to Instantly Relieve Doubt:

- I give myself permission to risk making a mistake.

- I am lovable through all my successes and failures, my mistakes and my victories.

- I open my heart to experiencing the result of this decision.

- I choose to experience any fear of the unknown as excitement about a new adventure.

- I trust that this choice or action brings forward whatever is in the highest and best good for all.

* * *

How Does Intuition Look on You?

Because we are unique, each person gets their intuitive information differently.

- Some people have a very strong gut feeling—literally they might have stomach pains when considering an option that doesn't fit.

- Some people hear voices.

- Others have visions.

- Some experience others emotions.

- I met one woman who would stop being able to smell out of one of her nostrils when something was off.

- Another woman gets a metal taste in her mouth when she needs to pay attention.

- Other people know things as if the answers just drop into their mind out of thin air.

- Some like me have a whole combination of ways information shows up.

There is no wrong way to experience your intuitive guidance. Your way will be unique to you. When you are open to receiving intuitive information, more of it will begin arriving. It's just up to you to begin noticing it however it comes.

Listening to your intuition is a bit like learning a new language. When I first started communicating directly with my guides I did not receive auditory messages. They would show me pictures of very complicated metaphors. It was a bit how some people describe their dreams. Interacting with them made things more confusing, not less confusing. That was until I learned how to translate their messages.

My partner at the time had a great idea, she suggested that since I could see the pictures clearly, why not give them a white board and have them write in English the explanation in ways I would understand.

Wow, that made all the difference. Seeing the words in my mind's eye eventually evolved to my hearing the words in my inner ear instead. There is still a ton of information that I miss or don't understand—but by keeping focused on improving all the time I allow myself to open to more opportunities to receive clearly.

* * *

WHY IS USING YOUR INTUITION IMPORTANT?
Intuition is often discussed as women's wisdom. And yes, if intellect is the masculine aspect, intuition is the feminine aspect. The issue is that there has been such an overvaluing

of intellect that we often deny that intuition is equally valid and valuable.

And when we do not consider intuition and inner wisdom, what happens is that we make choices, often lots of them, based on what our mind alone says is good. Our mind also holds all our old programming that we got from our parents and the culture at large and operates primarily based on outdated but subconscious survival strategies. Intuition takes into account the bigger picture.

✳ ✳ ✳

HOW TO GET STARTED USING YOUR INTUITION

1. **Start with your body.** More answers can be found there than in your mind. Tightness in your chest or belly, heaviness in your legs, or lightness and excitement in your head, all can indicate wisdom it would be helpful for you to acknowledge. Most of us ignore these indicators because we don't know how to translate them.

2. **Translate what you notice.** The basic guidance around what things mean is usually that when you check-in and you notice it feels light, energizing, or exciting, that's a strong positive for whatever you're deciding. If something feels heavy, dark, draining, tight, or uncomfortable, that's a negative indicator. Note that if you have a history of physical trauma, many people have learned not to trust their body because it is an unsafe, painful place to be. I know many people who are highly intuitive with this background, sometimes it requires more support to sort out what is fear from previous trauma and what is a true indicator of the current situation.

3. **Slow down before you make choices.** Intuition requires deep inner listening. Too often we are busy and have too much stimulus to notice what is going on with us at a more subtle level. So to make space for your intuition, stop and go inside and sit quietly and be with the question.

4. **Notice if something "doesn't feel right or good."** It is common to have some natural instinct. Often we then try to rationalize away why we shouldn't follow it. The data is real even if you can't explain it. Consider your intuitive insight with a heavier weight because your mind will attempt to talk you out of it.

REFLECT:

Describe one circumstance when you have had an intuitive nudge or gut feeling and followed it and this was helpful.

Describe one circumstance when you rationalized away your instinct or inner wisdom and it cost you.

How did the information, instinct, or knowing in each circumstance show up for you? Some sensation in your body? Some emotions? Certain thoughts? Be as specific as you can.

What was the difference between the two experiences when you followed your intuition and when you didn't?

IMPLEMENT:

What's one way you will commit to formally incorporating following your heart and intuition into your decision-making process?

How can this help you avoid (or recover from) feeling drained and burned out?

A YES OR A NO IS NOT FOUND
ON A PRO/CON LIST.

ONLY YOUR HEART AND YOUR INTUITION
WILL REVEAL THE ANSWERS THAT ARE
ALIGNED FOR YOU.

CHAPTER EIGHT:

OWN YOUR INNER GAME

WHEN I WAS TWENTY-ONE I HAD AN EMBARRASSING PROBlem. Warts.

It started with just one on one finger. It felt like something I wanted to hide. Who knows why warts would be such a big deal, but they were.

You're not supposed to get warts. Even as a little kid I knew that warts weren't good. Witches have warts. Which at the time meant somehow I was a bad or dirty person if I had them. I couldn't get the original to go away. And before I knew it I had a collection of them on a few different fingers. Then worse, on my face.

See, I have a signature nose itch. There are videos of me doing this in any performance when I was a little kid. It's completely a subconscious habit at this point, I regularly itch my nose (even when it doesn't itch) by running my right index finger underneath it from my fingertip to my first knuckle.

Guess where the wart was? On my index finger. And guess where the wart moved to? Yep. On the underside of my nose.

I tried cremes. I tried freezing them off at home. No use. I finally went to the dermatologist to get help.

For a sensitive person, having anything frozen off your body with liquid nitrogen isn't pretty. I cried every time. The first time I went by myself. It was awful. After that it was a little better when my partner went with and held my hand. The ones on my nose though, ohhhh—that really sucked.

But after three or four times doing this and seeing no improvement I didn't know what to do. Obviously this treatment wasn't helping, I needed to do something else—but I didn't know what.

I grew up with western medicine only, the philosophy that when something physical was going on you take a pill, cut it off, or in this case, freeze it off—that was *real* medicine. Anything else that didn't come from science was all hocus pocus. But since the *real* medicine wasn't working, I was willing at that point to consider other options.

Before we had met, my partner had become certified as a hypnotherapist which she had done as a side job for awhile. She'd told me some stories about her clients who had done everything from healing migraines, to stopping night terrors, and improving their golf swings.

On one hand I was fascinated, but when it came to me, the truth was hypnotherapy scared me. I didn't like the idea of what I perceived to be someone manipulating my mind.

But I was in a situation where I didn't know what to do anymore. So I bravely asked the question, "Honey, do you think hypnosis would help my warts go away?" She told me she didn't know, but that it was worth a try.

A couple days later, I laid down on the couch under a blanket. My eyes closed, she wooed me into a highly relaxed state talking very slowly with a calming voice.

From there, it was a complete black out to me. Still to this day I have no recollection whatsoever of what happened during that session. We've talked about it since and she doesn't even remember what suggestions she made to my subconscious mind.

What I do know is that I woke up feeling good, like I'd just had a restorative nap. And shock of all shocks, without any other intervention, all the embarrassing warts completely disappeared in the next month. Gone. Never to be seen again.

That experience made me take notice. I realized that there must be something else going on inside me that was not about just what was happening on a physical level.

Somehow, something mentally or emotionally influenced and maybe even created the experience of what was happening on the outside of me. And, by accessing my subconscious mind and telling it something different, I was able to heal and have a completely different experience.

That was the beginning of where my world started to change as I continued to learn more and more about the power of my inner game.

* * *

Here's What I've Learned Since Then
Not all warts are physical. They come in many forms.

We all have things that we're ashamed or embarrassed about or wish wasn't happening or hadn't happened in many areas of our lives. Some of these include:

- How much or how little money we make.

- Debt.

- Bankruptcy.

- Having inherited money instead of made it ourselves.

- Where we live or what kind of car we drive.

- Body image and health related issues.

- Physical, mental, emotional, or sexual abuse.

- Lying.

- Stealing.

- Cheating.

- Being cheated on.

- Hurting someone.

- Hurting ourselves.

- Suicidal thoughts or attempts.

- Lack of education or difficulty in school.

- Intelligence level.

- What arouses us sexually.

* * *

GETTING THE WARTS & ICKY FEELINGS TO GO AWAY

I'll give you a clue: the dermatologist isn't going to be any help with this one either. Whatever it is that we'd rather other people didn't know about is a clue that there's something going on underneath the surface in our inner game that is probably impacting more aspects of our life and business or work than we've even considered.

And until we resolve the programming we're running, just like replacing a line of code that operates a computer, that programming will continue to create the experience we want to hide or that we're not proud about.

This was the beginning of my looking for answers that go to the root of the issue versus just addressing the symptoms. It wasn't as though at that point I had things all figured out.

* * *

Failing to Own My Inner Game

One of the worst times when I completely failed to own the affect of my inner game didn't happen until years later. In 2007, I had taken a year off to coauthor an award-winning book with my then partner, Jennifer. Still it's one of the hardest things I have ever done. The book was about relationships, specifically about experiencing more love and joy in them and was based on things in our own experience worked.

Yet, when the book was completed, I still saw myself as a graphic designer. I wasn't an expert at anything. I wasn't perfect enough at anything we discuss in the book. From my viewpoint, she was the one with the wisdom and voice to share and yet both of our names were on the cover.

It was a project that we had done mostly together, yet mostly on our own. We wrote the book passing the drafts back and forth to one another. We had outside help with editing, but the design of the book was done by me, the illustrations done by me, the website and marketing promotions, all designed by me. We read books on book promotion and cobbled together a promotional strategy, running workshops at bookstores in our region that Jennifer organized.

Our intention at the time was to make our living helping people transform their relationships based on the book. Build it and people will come was the idea.

Except when we launched it, they didn't come. Over a year of work for both of us totally fell flat. We could barely enroll our friends into low cost trainings much less those we didn't know.

We weren't having fun. The two of us were arguing all the time. It was a highly stressful. Ironically, we were selling a product about bringing more love and joy into your relationships and your life and it was easily the most challenging time in our own relationship.

As much as I was great at marketing, I wasn't great at marketing *this*. As much as she was great at selling, she wasn't great at selling *this*. We didn't recognize the gaps in our skill sets and experience. We didn't see the places where we weren't living in alignment with the principles we were intent on teaching. We didn't invest in mentors who had done this type of work before and filled rooms for paid workshops successfully.

And importantly, we didn't address the space that I had personally moved into around leading workshops, a place where I felt like a big imposter.

I wasn't perfect enough. I wasn't expert enough to be leading anyone. I was terrified about getting things wrong on a public stage and what that would mean or prove about me. I didn't recognize the gifts and value of what I brought to the table. And I was completely resistant about being in that role.

Looking back at it now, no wonder people weren't attracted. After months of frustration and cancelled workshops, instead of getting help with what was happening internally and externally and refocusing our efforts, we moved onto other things.

We had heard from gurus who had been selling workshops for years that 2008, the year we had launched, was the worst for everyone. Even the known names weren't getting people to their workshops.

And so that became our story too: bad timing. Breaking up with this business was painful because we had invested so much time, energy, and money. Yet there was a big relief to do something else because we were both miserable and frustrated.

I went back to sitting behind the computer gift wrapping garbage where I was comfortably uncomfortable. I didn't like it, and it was what I knew. Leading a group was way outside my comfort zone. I had a hard time with the idea of Jennifer being a star without me, and yet I was terrified of putting myself out there and being vulnerable.

I often wonder if I had addressed the inner game issues that were clearly impacting both my and our collective success if things might have turned out differently?

* * *

Inner Game Aspects that Were in the Way

- I told myself I had to be perfect, that no one would perceive me as an expert or leader because I was too young or because I was gay and most of the people I believed the work could help were straight and they wouldn't relate to me.

- I told myself that I couldn't make a mistake. That making mistakes was essentially unlovable.

- I also felt like an imposter, why would anyone want to follow me?

- I didn't believe in investing in support unless it was absolutely something I couldn't do myself. Instead, do everything you can on your own.

- I believed that because others were having trouble with sales, that meant it should my story too.

- And because I didn't acknowledge all that was happening for me or get some support to do something about it, the business I was attempting to launch with my partner didn't achieve the result I wanted.

* * *

Look Inside First

Obviously a lot has changed since then. When I'm not getting the results I'm interested in, the first place I look now is in what's going on with me. Am I subconsciously sabotaging this in some way? Am I not aligned with what I'm creating?

This came up most recently where in my business I wasn't reaching the revenue goal I had in mind. It didn't seem like an outrageous goal. The trouble was, I wasn't even coming close to reaching it. In fact, I was going backwards. I'd stopped making almost any money at all.

When I looked inward more closely and teased out what it would mean to meet that goal, what I realized is that I had tied the revenue goal to what would happen next when I met it. I would be traveling more, spending months at a time working with clients online during the middle of the week and spending the weekends exploring different destinations in Europe, Asia, and South America.

On one hand, that seemed like a dream come true, right, no problems there. Except when I probed further and asked myself the question of what would it mean to travel more and the answer that I heard was, "I wouldn't get my touch needs met," I knew I had found my answer.

See, my primary language for both giving and receiving love is touch. If you haven't read *The 5 Love Languages* book by Gary Chapman, it's well worth the read and can shed a lot of light on frustrations in your love relationships if your partner(s) express or receive love differently than you do.

I was single and dating at the time—and the relationships I was developing were all local in Minneapolis. None of the folks had very flexible jobs or could travel in the way that I envisioned.

I was getting my touch needs met so long as I was located in the Twin Cities. But as soon as I started traveling by myself? Nope, not anymore. Not being touched can mean I feel physically vacant—it brings me back into my body. When lack of touch goes on for much more than a week I start to feel like part of me is missing.

Yet, I had no vision of being able to travel while getting those needs met. And because I had tied my revenue goal to the travel, I was subconsciously preventing myself from reaching the goal as a survival strategy.

Staying put in Minnesota is how I'd get my touch needs met. If I made more money and traveled more, I wouldn't. I now know that relationships and giving and receiving loving touch specifically are clearly far more valuable than money to me on a few different levels. Enough so that I would subconsciously sabotage my progress to make sure those primary needs are met.

When I realized the issue keeping me from the goal was more about how to get my touch needs met while traveling, this allowed me to finally begin getting traction toward that income goal and make more money.

MENTORS HELP YOU SEE YOUR INNER GAME CLEARLY

My experience has been that when we work with a mentor who can see our inner game clearly is when the goodies that we are blind to ourselves come to light.

One of my clients has several advanced degrees, even a doctorate. She kept feeling the need to get more and more training. Yet it wasn't until she owned that she had been subconsciously seeking her father's approval to prove that she was good enough that she realized that who she is already was enough. Another initial after her name didn't make her any more or less worthy of anyone's love. She stopped looking for evidence of her father's approval and started doing work that fed her personally and professionally. She's much happier, not burned out anymore, and more effective as a result.

Another of my clients said she wanted to meet the love of her life. At the same time she kept getting sucked into a relationship with someone who wasn't available. It wasn't until my client owned the fact that she was deathly afraid of breaking up with someone because she didn't want to inflict pain on anyone that things changed.

She recognized that the safe place for her was in caring for the other person and ignoring her own wants and needs. She finally ended the relationship and resolved to hold out for what she wanted. In the meantime, she practiced better self-care and gave herself her own time, love, and attention. Only then did she start meeting more available, openhearted people.

The things we are afraid of, the things we are embarrassed about, those are the things that often keep us from creating whatever it is that we want.

When we bring those things to light, when we acknowledge what we perceive as shortcomings and love ourselves anyway, that's when shifts start to happen easily and progress begins to be noticed.

REFLECT:

What is one goal or something that you've struggled with achieving or creating in your life that is still important to you now?

What do you tell yourself it would mean to achieve that goal?

In order to achieve this goal who would you have to be that you aren't right now?

What would you have to be willing to give up?

What would you have to be willing to receive?

What have your answers to these questions revealed about your inner game that you could choose to own and address to make progress toward your goal right now?

IMPLEMENT:

What next step toward your goal relative to your inner game are you committed to taking this week?

The story you tell yourself on the inside creates the reality you experience on the outside.

What needs attention in your inner game?

CHAPTER NINE:

INVEST IN WHAT YOU VALUE MOST

I STOOD WITH MY ARMS FULLY OUTSTRETCHED LIKE A BIRD teetering on a rock outcropping no bigger than two feet put together at the edge of a cliff overlooking the valley below.

Any misstep and I could tumble a long way down the cliff into the ravine. It felt like I was flying. Or at least, that I could fly.

I lifted one foot a la Karate kid so I was fully balancing on one leg. My knee shook a little and I felt the reassuring grip of the shaman's hands around my waist as he spotted me from behind. Perched at the top of Machu Picchu, I welcomed feelings of freedom and power back into my life.

At the time, this was the most expensive trip financially I had ever taken. It was two weeks with a small group of spiritual seekers lead by a shaman in Peru. And still to this day it was one of the most important in my personal development.

I walked on red hot coals without being burned and saw beyond my perception of my own physical limitations. I learned how to intuitively read people's energy off their metal jewelry. I meditated in sacred places and felt deeply connected to the earth. And I learned that people do not destroy things out of any ill will, only through their lack of consciousness.

I had friends who claimed they couldn't afford a decent vacation, certainly none like this. Yet I watched them invest money in new vehicles or buy more expensive homes and other toys every couple years. This told me that they hadn't made travel a priority in their lives.

And that's just it, it's rarely about whether you can afford something, it's about whether it's a priority for you. For me, I'd rather take another awesome trip than drive the newest car. And as such, I've always driven vehicles that were between 9–25 years old. My trusty Subaru gets me from point A to point B safely and reliably in a comfortable climate controlled environment.

It camps well, hauls a cool find from a garage sale, and has helped me move more than once. I don't need any fancy electronic gadgets in my car. The vehicle barely depreciates and gets reasonable gas mileage.

If I wanted to sell it today, I could get nearly the amount I paid for it two years ago. And since I live in a neighborhood where I usually walk instead of drive, this would hardly change my life. Having a car is a convenience, not a necessity.

We choose how we invest our time, energy, and money. Sometimes it feels like we *have* to spend time or money on certain expenses. Though for the most part we choose where we live. We choose whether we drive a car or ride the bus. We choose whether we work at a job or in a particular business. Everything is a choice.

WHERE ARE YOU INVESTING YOUR RESOURCES?

The evidence of how we spend our time, energy, and money is all around us. And when things aren't going the way we wish in any particular area, one of the first things to do is check-in on where we are out of alignment with how we are investing those resources.

For example, in a year where my business was not doing so well, where was my time and energy being invested? Turned out it was in my personal relationships. My dating life was my highest priority and was going very well. My business hadn't been getting much time and attention and so I wasn't seeing the results I wanted.

Was it possible to do both—be successful in my personal relationships and my business? Probably. But at the time, clearly not for me. Or at least that wasn't the choice I was making.

When I moved cross-country from California to Minnesota I felt so ungrounded I needed to invest time in recreating a sense of home for myself. And that meant investing time in romantic relationships and friendships that would support me. It was definitely a much higher priority than my business and it was my way of making home.

And you know what, I still gave myself such a hard time that my business wasn't moving forward in the way that I thought I wanted. I desired forward progress but I couldn't seem to summon more consistent energy or effort towards it.

That was until I realized that I was simply investing my time in what mattered most to me. And until I was aligned with doing both, investing in both my personal life *and* my business, nothing different was going to happen.

WHAT I VALUE MOST IN MY LIFE

1. Freedom: My personal development & evolution.

2. Love, intimacy, & connection with people I love.

3. Quality of life.
   (Living somewhere I enjoy, regular travel, having unique experiences one can only have as a human.)

4. My health.

5. Making an impact in the world.

Based on being aligned with my choices and investing in what I value most, I could only grow my business when I wasn't stressed out and overwhelmed. Anytime I got stressed out and overwhelmed, I was out of alignment with creating the business that I wanted.

My top values are freedom and enjoyment of life, time for intimacy and connection with people I love, and my health. None of those work if I am stressed out and overwhelmed and they are higher priorities.

My business mostly falls into number five which is making an impact in the world. Quality of life to me mostly doesn't have to do with work, it has to do with having free time to do whatever I want when I want.

You'll notice that in some ways the first four values are very *me* centric. It comes from the idea that I need to fill my own bucket first before I can be available to do bigger good in the world. They are more localized to my personal experience.

When those are handled well, then I am more well resourced and capable of making a bigger impact in the world. When my personal world feels out of balance, it impacts my ability to contribute.

THE WHY MATTERS

As professionals who set goals we are intent on achieving, it can be easy to get priorities out of order. Remembering the *why* of what we're doing and making sure we're setting things up to support that why is the essence of doing things in an aligned way.

But particularly when we are people-pleasers, this can get complicated. For example, my client Sarah ran a very successful marketing company. Her motivation behind doing it was to support her family. When we first started working together her stress and anxiety topped the charts at a nine out of ten.

She worked long hours. The time she spent in the evening relaxing involved sitting on the couch with her husband in front of the TV with her cell phone answering client emails. She hadn't taken a vacation without working, ever. Time spent with her step-daughters and husband was constantly interrupted by calls and emails from work.

The whole reason she was working so hard was to support her family. And yet, what the people in her life most wanted was her and she wasn't really there with them. She never could give the people she loved her full attention because she was always working or worried about work.

Through our work together she was able to communicate different expectations with clients. She set regular hours for returning email and answering calls instead of being available 24/7. That was scary because she was afraid she would lose clients. She did it anyway, and she was both surprised and thrilled she didn't lose anyone.

In fact, she started charging for rush projects and last minute changes, so any inconvenience to her actually made her more money. And it made clients evaluate how important it was to have that last minute change or get things completed quickly. Most of the time it turned out it wasn't worth paying extra for those services.

I challenged her to have more quality time with her husband. Their favorite impact of our work together was their weekly date they started taking together. Both of them would set aside their cell phones and just focus on one another. And evenings on the couch became their cell phone free zone.

She even set up her staff to handle things well enough in her absence that she took a cell phone free vacation to celebrate her step-daughter's graduation. It was a first and it impressed her whole family. They loved having her there.

The impact of these changes also had a huge impact on how she felt day-to-day. Her stress and anxiety levels dropped significantly—to 0–3 out of ten, easily a 70% decrease.

And because she was investing in what mattered most to her, she felt great about herself. No more guilt about not being present in her relationships that she had started her business to support in the first place.

She actually found she was able to serve her clients better because she felt more focused and relaxed when she was doing their work. Everybody in this scenario wins.

When you make aligned choices and invest in what you value most there isn't part of you playing the "yeah but" game.

—yeah, but you're abandoning your family.
—yeah, but you're not making the money you want.
—yeah, but you'll be letting down your clients.

Reality check: It is not possible to invest in all of your values at the same time. Some are higher priorities than others. And it's a matter of deciding which you are going to set down so that you can achieve something instead of nothing when you spread yourself too thin.

REFLECT:

What are your top 3–5 values and priorities in your life?

How are you currently investing your time, money, and energy relative to those values and priorities?

In what ways do you spend your resources on things you don't care as much about as your highest priorities?

Is there anything you are ready to let go of that distracts from your highest priorities?

IMPLEMENT:

What commitment are you ready to make to re-focus your investment of time, energy, and resources on what you value most? How will you make progress on that this week?

Feeling energized & satisfied by life requires investing time, money, & energy in alignment with your highest values & priorities.

THE S.A.S.S. SYSTEM:

SUSTAINABLE

CHAPTER TEN:

WORK IN PARTNERSHIP
WITH YOUR BODY

I used to pull all-nighters. I'd have a big project to complete for a design client and a deadline to have it done and sometimes that's what it would take. Last minute changes the day before something goes to the printer? On the outside I'd tell the client with a smile, "Oh of course, sure, I can do that." Inside I'd be groaning, "Uggggh. Looks like I'm not sleeping. Again."

As a freelancer usually after the project was delivered I'd have a day or two of downtime to do my best to catch up. I was lucky.

I had colleagues who worked for ad agencies across town. Sometimes they would pull all-nighters too. The difference was that they worked ridiculous hours all the time. They were tired all the time. They never had a chance to catch up. Even weekends they were usually working.

Eventually they got burned out and quit. They'd consider themselves lucky if they didn't wind up with adrenal fatigue, digestive issues, or some other health problem.

The reality is that working all the time and crazy hours takes a toll. It hampers our social life. Friends? What are those? It costs us quality time with any partner or family. And it really messes up our health.

It took me over a week to recover fully from pulling one all-nighter. There were a couple times I did it twice in the same week, and as soon as the project was delivered and the over-drive was relieved, I got sick.

The idea that you must work hard to get ahead runs strong in our culture. Somehow ignoring the needs of our body is considered evidence of being strong. And as women we are conditioned to put everyone else's needs above our own—so somehow sacrificing ourselves and our bodies is built into our DNA.

Yet this is not a sustainable way to operate if you want to be as effective as possible long-term. Caring for your body as a true partner and avoiding running it into the ground is an essential part of efficient achievement.

* * *

Our Body Enables Our Achievement

Our body is the vehicle through which we are able to work and contribute. And if our energy becomes distracted and drained by a heath issue, that means we have less energy to make the impact we would like to make in the world both personally and professionally. And we miss out on a whole lot of fun too.

In no way is it weak to listen to your body and honor what it needs. It takes a ton of strength to stand up to the culture and take care of yourself instead of pretending that your pain or exhaustion or other discomfort or need isn't there.

Many times, we face disappointing someone else by admitting we have needs too. You are not a robot. It's perfectly okay to have needs and desires. Just because you're a super achiever and people in your life have particular expectations about how you usually are, doesn't magically mean that you can keep up with that if you don't take care of yourself. The prescription for relief is simple.

* * *

Listen to What Your Body Needs

- Are you are tired? Sleep.

- Hungry? Eat.

- Need some downtime by yourself? Get a babysitter.

- Stiff or uncomfortable? Dance, walk, or move.

- Neck and shoulder pain? Get a massage.

- Thirsty? Drink.

- Overwhelmed by a request? Say NO.

* * *

Every Body is Different

Do what works for you instead of following someone else's plan that works for them. A perfect example of this is Michelle Obama. Love her or hate her, she's a high achiever who has always had a ton on her plate.

In an interview with *Prevention* magazine she discusses how she would get up at five in the morning to feed her daughters when they were infants. She hadn't been prioritizing exercise and she realized that if she was willing to get up that early for others that she would be well served to make a commitment to do it for herself. Exercise made her feel better.

Her revised routine included getting up 4:30 a.m. to get in her work out. When she got up and out early that also meant her husband would handle the first feeding.

She reflects it is important to, "Do what makes you feel good, because there will always be someone who thinks you should do it differently. Whether your choices are hits or misses, at least they're your own."

Personally, I'm not an early morning person and the first thing on my self-care list is sleep. So if I were to take on Michelle's schedule I'd be likely to feel off. And that's exactly the point. Each of our bodies is unique. What works for her doesn't have to work for me and what works for me might not work for you.

Listening to what your unique body needs and making choices in alignment with it is the most essential part of supporting your health. When you support your own wellness you set the stage for higher achievement because you're not wasting time or energy being sick or tired.

If we don't take care of ourselves in the way that works best for us and instead we run ourselves ragged, it eventually catches up with us.

* * *

The Heath & Productivity Cost

Ohio State University researcher, Allard Dembe, has found that for women there is a strong relationship between working long hours, particularly over fifty hours per week, and developing early onset heart disease, cancer, arthritis, and diabetes. Based on previous research he has learned that women juggle more family demands than their male counterparts so that when they work longer hours they face more stress. That stress can translate into dis-ease.

"One in four women die from heart disease and one in thirty women die from breast cancer. Heart disease is the number one killer of women," Dr. Martha Gulati explains to *Newsmax* about her study done with Kavita Sharma M.D.

Their study notes that overall death rate from heart disease in the U.S. has dropped by thirty percent from 1998 to 2008. But rates among women younger than fifty-five years old are still on the rise. Women under fifty who have a heart attack are twice as likely as men to die.

We all have a capacity. And when we continuously run on empty with high adrenaline hormones in a high-paced, high stress environment, something's got to give. And usually, that's our health. Each of us has our weak spot whether that's our heart, our immune system, or our nervous system where pain can show up.

Myself, I struggled with chronic back pain for a long time. When things were out of balance I could stay out of pain if I got massage once a week. And now that things are more in balance I stay comfortable getting a massage once a month.

According to the National Institute of Health, lost productivity due to chronic pain costs businesses $11.6–$12.7 billion annually.

Recognizing the Trickle-Down & Capacity of Your Team

Our effectiveness and productivity naturally declines when we don't feel well. And the same can be said for your team. Are your team members healthy, alert, and energetic? Or are they stressed, struggling with burn out, and just trying to get through the day?

Your team is the body of your business. Know that whatever you model as you care for yourself trickles down to them.

Do you have a habit of working all hours or powering through even though you're exhausted? If so, intentionally or unintentionally, that's the message you're sending of what you expect from them.

24/7 availability doesn't work as a sustainable, healthy business model. If your staff is feeling burned out because they haven't stopped to care for themselves that means their productivity will go down the drain too.

And it doesn't matter whether their stressors are personal or professional. All stress runs together. For maximum effectiveness they need to take care of their bodies, get enough rest, and take regular breaks from work. Performing at peak productivity requires treating oneself like a star athlete—focusing on basics like food, water, rest, movement, and mindset.

What habits do you and your team have? True leadership isn't about showing strength by ignoring what's happening with you physically, mentally, and emotionally and powering through. That is the old paradigm that makes people sick.

* * *

How to Lead By Example & Promote Healthy Living

1. Have recess together. Get out and walk with your team. Have competitions for the most steps taken in a day. In

some cases you can even have walk and talk meetings. Even virtual meetings can offer a break from sitting and include push-ups, dancing, or a few minutes of activity.

2. Have weekly whole food potlucks or do 30-day challenges like Whole30® or paleo programs.

3. Take vacations where you unplug. By modeling this and not expecting staff to be available while they're on vacation it encourages them to do the same.

4. Take sick days or mental health days as you need them. Don't wait until you can't get out of bed. When you do this you show your team members that it's okay to take care of themselves. Send team members home who are not well mentally or physically, don't hold this against them later.

5. Start your day with meditation or yoga or have a meditation or mindfulness break during the day. If you have an office, create a space where someone can have a peaceful moment of reflection when needed. This might be a small quiet retreat room with a fountain or a recliner in the corner with headphones playing relaxing music. Use this space yourself too.

6. Work regular hours that leaves room for rest and downtime. Your downtime might be evenings or weekends unless that's the busy time in what you do. If weekends are prime time work hours, make sure you choose other days to rest and reset.

7. Make sure that if you do choose to send team members messages because you are inspired during non-work hours that you indicate at the top of the message that

you don't expect them to get back to you until the next business day. Honor their time away from work as necessary and helpful to their health and productivity.

8. Make health one of the priorities you track in your business. Set a related organizational target which might be the total number of steps everyone walks in a day or reducing missed days of work or limiting evening work or overtime. Ask each team member to choose how they will contribute to achieving that goal and ask them what support they need to do it.

By being a living example of listening to your body, eating healthfully, and taking breaks from work, you step into true leadership. When you do this and develop policies and a culture that encourage your team to do the same, the result is more sustainable for everyone because they are happier, healthier, and more productive.

REFLECT:

Describe your relationship with your body and how you typically work in partnership with it or not right now:

What current habits help you perform at the highest level?

What current habits detract from your performance?

How does what you're modeling affect your team or family? (If you have either one.)

IMPLEMENT:

What's one step you're committed to taking this week that would improve your partnership with your body?

CARING FOR YOUR BODY LIKE A WELL-LOVED FRIEND IS FAR MORE EFFICIENT THAN DEALING WITH THE CONSEQUENCES OF IGNORING IT.

CHAPTER ELEVEN:

BUILD IN BREAKS

I'D BEEN WORKING HARD ALL DAY. FRUSTRATED WITH THE project and feeling like I was forcing things, I knew I needed to stop banging my head against the wall. So I laced up my sneakers and pulled on a jacket, tucking my keys, wallet, and cell phone away in my pockets, and headed out for some inspiration on a walk in my neighborhood.

The air was crisp and the leaves were just starting to turn and drop. My feet crunched the fallen seeds on the sidewalk. I could hear the cars from the busy adjacent street. I started to drift off in a daydream for a moment and I glanced down, igniting a moment of panic as I narrowly avoided stepping squarely in poop a lovely neighbor had left on the sidewalk.

I relaxed again, grateful and relieved to have avoided the landmine. And from that point I was more mindful to look down consistently as my mind floated.

I don't know why the answers come through so clearly when I walk, they just do. If I walk out the door with a question, I walk back in with the answer.

This day was no different. I focused on being present and breathing and enjoying the beauty of fall. And as I started to open my inner ears to deep listening, the messages about where I was stuck on this project floated in.

Early on in my career this would've been the last approach I'd take to moving a project forward quickly. The few times where I've taken contract gigs that had me working in an office cubicle I'd watch resentfully as the smokers trickled out for their withdrawl-driven breaks.

Was I the only one in the office who thought they were slackers? Everyone else was working, did they think they were better than all of us? Part of me was jealous and wanted to feel good about taking those breaks too. But I didn't. I'd learned that powering through and working harder was *the way*.

I've realized a few things since then that these smokers had right. Taking breaks actually helps us be more productive.

* * *

THE EFFECTS OF BREAKS ON PRODUCTIVITY

A 2011 study at the University of Illinois at Urbana-Champaign by Alejandro Lleras found that when focusing on a task, taking a brief break every hour allowed subjects to maintain performance over a longer time than those who did not take breaks. Lleras reports that the drop in performance happens when we become habituated to the task and then stop paying attention to it.

This is similar to how we process other stimulus that remains constant over time. Our brain simply erases it as unimportant. For example, if we sit somewhere for awhile, we eventually stop noticing how the chair feels against our lower back and legs.

The same happens for a project that we try to focus on too long. Taking a break allows the task to become new in our awareness again.

The trouble is that we live in a culture where we continuously push to do more, to be more, and to have more. And there's some serious urgency about it. So it's no surprise that breaks, vacations, and downtime are often thought about as wasted time and people are reluctant to take them.

A 2013 *New York Times* article by Tony Schwartz cites that more than one-third of employees eat lunch at their desks and more that fifty percent expect to work on their vacations.

We see that the prevailing work ethic in companies rewards those who work continuously. And this is despite the fact that the research shows that working harder and longer can actually make someone less productive and effective overall.

Spending more time at work tends to contribute to having less time for sleep which can dramatically decrease performance. A Swedish study published in the *Journal of Occupational Health Psychology* indicates that sleeping less than six hours per night is the biggest predictor of job related burn-out. And Harvard researchers estimate that sleep deprivation costs U.S. businesses $63.2 billion in lost productivity every year.

* * *

Breaks are Better than Overtime for Productivity

Working overtime isn't the answer to higher performance. Taking regular breaks from work is.

Schwartz' *New York Times* article goes on to describe an internal study done by Ernst & Young in 2006. The research indicated that for each additional ten hours of vacation employees took their performance reviews from supervisors improved by eight percent. Those who vacationed more were also more likely to stay with the company.

Of course this isn't exactly the whole story. Working too little will impact performance negatively too. But as achievers we're more likely to work too much than we are to work too little. We've been conditioned to think that there's not enough time to take breaks, which leaves us stuck.

The one thing we're most afraid of is not doing enough, not being enough. So of course, we're resistant to stopping and resting and doing less even for a moment—and even if it's what would make us more productive overall.

* * *

BREAKS FUEL CREATIVITY

The other thing to consider is that a break can also serve as new inspiration and creative fuel. Just because you're not officially working doesn't mean your subconscious isn't actively in creative mode while you're resting, playing, and enjoying yourself. Vacations have inspired many profitable ideas.

According to Shaun Thomson, CEO of Sandler Training, in a recent study of 1000 successful businesses that have been in business more than five years, nearly one in five had their inspiration while the entrepreneur was on vacation.

There is something about the magic of an extended break that allows us to think differently. We're out of our regular environment having conversations with those who we'd never encounter any other way. Changing up our routine creates fertile ground for new ideas.

Oᴜᴛ-ᴏꜰ-ᴛʜᴇ-Bᴏx Iɴsᴘɪʀᴀᴛɪᴏɴ Fᴏᴜɴᴅ Aᴡᴀʏ ꜰʀᴏᴍ ᴛʜᴇ Oꜰꜰɪᴄᴇ

- Lin Manuel Miranda came up with the idea for the musical, *Hamilton*, while on vacation.

- Bianca Forzano took breaks from her corporate job at PricewaterhouseCoopers to kitesurf. In doing so she realized there wasn't a secure sports bikini on the market that was stylish too. So she launched the Italian made line of BiancaBikinis that stay on in the water.

- The inspiration for the groundbreaking filters on Instagram came to founder Kevin Systrom while walking on the beach in Mexico.

- Starbucks CEO Howard Schultz came up with the idea to make Starbucks part of everyone's morning ritual and sense of community in the 1980s based on a trip he took to Verona, Italy.

Margaret Groves, an ecommerce consultant from Engineered Process Improvement, told me about a time when she had a breakthrough idea while on a trip to Idaho.

She was taking some vacation time in part to attend a family member's memorial. After the day's activities she and her partner and a couple of his relatives headed off on a short drive to relax at a local hot springs.

The conversation in the car was relaxed and drifted to how beautiful Idaho was. It was late, about 9:30 at night as they arrived to the hot springs. Margaret remembered, "The hot springs was run by a old hippy woman. There were tiki torches everywhere, almost like a resort. There was a lot of infrastructure, which as a girl who enjoys room service makes me feel better."

They got settled and relaxed, soaking in the warm, sulph-
uric water under the stars and sharing stories about family.
At one point she and her partner were sitting just the two of
them. Shawn was mid-story when suddenly Margaret looked
at him surprised, as if the answer had dropped out of the sky,
and said, "You know what my client needs?"

Startled about being interrupted, he erupted, "What??? I
was telling you something!"

She continued, "Yes babe, I know, I was listening. But you
know what my client needs, he needs a banner on the website."

The big idea she had that night was for a client who was an
online tool retailer. Their tool buying clientele wasn't very web
savvy. Customers liked being able to call and chat with the
company's charming service reps. But just because they could
call, didn't mean they wanted to call.

In that moment in the hot springs, "I realized that 80% of
the questions were about bits and blades sizes," something she
explained was actually faster for the customer to look up on
their own on the company website.

Her big idea was to add a banner at the top of the site that
read, "New: find your bits and blades by size right from the
drop down menu."

Margaret continued, "This was not some innovative filter that we had just implemented. Not at all. But I figured it
would get people's attention. My client already had this really
great website where you could filter by the kind of material
you were trying to cut, by the size, the thickness of the saw
blades, all these different things, but it wasn't being utilized."

She quickly implemented the change and the numbers
spoke for themselves. Sales grew about 40%. Phone calls were
reduced by one third. Each sales representative literally saved
one hour per day. With three on staff that was sixty hours a

month total. At $30 per hour, that was $1,800 per month that could be invested in other things.

Margaret's story is not an anomaly. When we take breaks, our subconscious keeps churning behind the scenes, actively solving our most challenging questions.

* * *

Scheduling Your Breakthroughs

You've likely had experiences yourself when you're on a walk, in the shower, or on a trip and the solution you've been looking for suddenly drops into your mind as if out of thin air. The answer seems so obvious, but when you were looking for it consciously you couldn't see it at all.

Even if you don't come back from a vacation with big ideas, a 2011 Intuit study revealed that 82% of small business owners who took a vacation had an increase in performance when they returned to work. When you're inspired and rested, that inspiration and motivation can positively affect your team's performance too.

* * *

The Formula that Works for Building in Breaks

There isn't any universal magic answer here. It's about experimenting and figuring out what works best for you.

Research from multiple sources suggests that working in sixty to ninety minute chunks and then taking five to ten minute breaks helps you maintain optimal performance. Note that just going to the bathroom and running back doesn't count, you need to really give yourself a chance to focus on something that seems delightfully non-productive for a few minutes.

Another option, the Pomodoro Technique,® was developed as a time management strategy by Francesco Cirillo. With this strategy you set a timer for twenty-five minutes and work intently. Then when the timer rings, take a three to five minute break. After four of these, take a longer fifteen to thirty minute break. There are several apps you can use to streamline this, though the timer you already have on your phone works too.

* * *

Build in Recovery Time

Each day, make sure that the amount of time you spend working leaves you enough time to adequately rest and recover. To do this you'll need to pay close attention to what helps you feel balanced. If you don't feel rested, you aren't.

When planning my work days I tend to think in terms of how much time I need to rest and recover. I need at least an hour in the morning after I wake up, then at the end of the day an hour for dinner and four hours of downtime before eight or nine hours of sleep in order to feel balanced. For me, sleep is one thing that if I skimp on I always pay for later.

That means my work day can be as long as ten hours for me to stay in balance, no more. Yet if I pull a ten hour day more than three days a week, I'll start to get exhausted. During the downtime between working I don't answer emails or other messages.

You'll need to identify and know what your limits are too. Different people need to sleep for different amounts and this may vary through their lives so build your schedule based on where you are now. And make sure you have clear times when you are not available by cell phone and not thinking about work so you can have the recovery time you need.

BUILD BREAKS INTO YOUR ROUTINE

Daily:
Experiment with a productivity system that keeps you focused and in top form with small breaks throughout the day.

Weekly:
Make sure you take at least one full day off, better two or three if you can swing it. Experts on labor speculate that even though Europeans take as much as double or more the vacation time that Americans do, it doesn't affect their work performance. When people spend less time at their desk they just waste less time with what they need to get done.

Every 3-6 Months:
Take at least a one-week vacation where you completely set down your professional responsibilities. And the more you can also set down your personal responsibilities of taking care of others during those times, the more quickly you will reset yourself and fill your tank.

* * *

STAY IN YOUR MOST EFFECTIVE STATE
To perform at optimum levels, build-in breaks and schedule your days in ways that you stay fresh, inspired, and energized. Encourage your team to do the same. That way most often you'll all be in your most productive and effective states.

REFLECT:

How much sleep do you need to feel rested? How much do you get?

What times of the day are you officially resting and recovering and not available by cell phone? Meal times? Evenings? Weekends? Set your schedule.

In what ways would you improve your effectiveness if you built more breaks into your daily activities?

When was your last vacation, and when is your next one scheduled?

What support would you need to take an entirely work-free vacation every 3–6 months?

IMPLEMENT:

What one step are you are committed to taking starting now to build more breaks into your schedule?

BREAKS INSPIRE BREAKTHROUGHS.
WHEN IS YOUR NEXT ONE?

CHAPTER TWELVE:

WELCOME SUPPORT

"Do you build websites?"

"YES," I answered, knowing full well I had done this in design college years ago and never since. I knew I could update my skills to current standards and deliver something great for her.

"Okay, I like your work and I'd like you to build me a website then. How much would you charge me for that?"

"I'll need to run some numbers on what I would recommend, then I'll put together a quote for you."

And so it began. I learned early to follow the money. It was far easier to get more business from an existing client than it was to generate a new one. So if what they needed was close enough to something that I already knew how to do, my answer was YES, I did that.

Copy writing? YES. Copy Editing? YES. Photography? YES. Web Design? YES. Product Design? YES. Trade Show Booth Design? YES. SEO? YES. Video Production? YES. Audio Editing? YES.

There were a couple upsides to this. For one, I was constantly expanding my skill set and clients continued to get great work without having to search for what they needed, deepening their relationship with me. I never pretended to be an expert in anything beyond design. I was smart and a great strategic thinker and they knew it.

And because clients trusted me to deliver a great product, they chose to work with me even though I had no experience doing some of the marketing projects they requested.

The downside to this was that I developed a very wide skill set and in many of these areas I became as competent as professionals who were specialists in that area alone. This made it harder for me to hand off projects or parts of projects to others—because I could consistently do a better job myself.

I was a full-blown perfectionist, so details I caught seemed to slip by others. And that was frustrating. So most of the time I just didn't bother passing things off to others, even those who worked for me when I could've.

It set me up for years of doing everything myself. Years of feeling unsupported and as though I was doing everything alone. Most of the time, I was.

* * *

WORKING IN YOUR GENIUS ZONE

If you asked me what my genius zone is, as much as I have many skills and talents, my greatest gift besides learning new things quickly is as a visionary and strategic thinker.

I'm able to look at a complicated situation with clarity and see several ways to resolve something. I see straight to the heart of people, and I understand instantly what's really happening even when they barely tell me what's going on.

Your genius zone includes the things you do easily, effortlessly, brilliantly, and joyfully. They don't feel like work. They can even feel fun.

For me, talking about ideas and coming up with new possibilities is totally energizing, joyful, and exciting—so this is my genius zone. But when it comes to the actual implementation of those ideas, I'm bored in the first twenty minutes.

Finishing a project when my role has included implementation has always been a struggle. I did it, and it wasn't fun. Production and implementation tasks are exhausting by comparison to the creative part of the project.

Turns out, had I chosen to get more support with those aspects that felt more taxing to me so that I could focus on creating the inspiration and ideas, I would've made more money in my design business. I also would've enjoyed my business instead of hating it.

Instead, my success was limited to my own available time because I couldn't leverage anyone else's. And I wound up constantly exhausted and always flirting with the edge of burn out.

Now I see what I missed before. Stick with my genius zone and what I do best. And whenever possible, delegate and get support with everything else.

* * *

DESIGNING LIFE & WORK WITH SUPPORT IN MIND

A perfect example of this was in choosing the system to manage my business finances. Dealing with financial details is not my thing at all. Why did I choose Quickbooks Online? Because it lives in the cloud not on my computer so that my remote bookkeeper, my accountant, and I all have easy access to it no matter where we are in the world. It is a simple system designed with support in mind.

Designing our lives and businesses with support in mind is a new concept for many women, even those in leadership roles. It's because we were socialized to be the ones who are supporters, not the ones who are supported.

This leaves many of us in situations where we don't know how or where or when would be appropriate to ask for support. Sometimes we do too much ourselves and don't feel good about delegating tasks that would be better handled by someone with a different or more limited skill set.

Why does this happen? Because we never learned how to be good at receiving support. What I now know is that if you have a big vision for how you want to impact the world, you can't go it alone. The bigger your vision, the more support you'll need in order to achieve it. Hold too tightly and try to do it all yourself and you'll not only burn out, you'll limit your effectiveness and impact.

* * *

DELEGATE ACTIVITIES OUTSIDE YOUR GENIUS ZONE

Getting comfortable with receiving support and delegating those things outside your genius zone is essential to success as a leader.

Deborah Gleason, lead consultant from The Information Tamer, told me, "I try to think of delegation as more empowerment. It's not about giving away tasks." She spends her days helping companies wrangle their inventory and understand data in their business.

Instead, she explained, it's more about finding a better fit for a project. She noted that as a senior level executive who knows strategy, she's going to be successful doing different things than a young person early in their career. And by giving that young person tasks they are capable of doing, "I'm going to be more successful by freeing myself up…[sic]…and getting onto more strategic work."

She told me about a young intern that had been working for them that was struggling to find his place. He'd needed a lot of check-ins and reassurance. She decided she was going to make him responsible for a whole project, something from beginning to end.

Deborah gave him group of products that she wanted the intern to liquidate and explained the guidelines for how she wanted him to do it. And of course, she encouraged him ask her questions when he got stuck.

The intern took it and ran with it. It was as if he had been sleeping and woke up. He got excited learning about mark downs and how to improve sales. And the best part Deborah celebrated, "I didn't have to think about it anymore! I got to move onto coming up with better strategy to market the business and buy new products to get more revenue coming in the door."

The end result was that the intern became far more engaged and the company had revenue coming in directly from his efforts. She continued, "But it was also a relief to me. Because it was a task that took a lot of time that I could never dedicate to this project. I could only give it ten minutes or fifteen minutes in between meetings. Whereas he could focus on it. And it turned him into a much more engaged employee."

In delegation, everyone wins. In a leadership role you win because your time is freed up to do other things. The person you're delegating to has work they're getting paid to do and potentially an opportunity to expand their skill set. They may even improve the process along the way. And your company wins in improved efficiency because the right people doing the tasks they are best suited to do means everything gets done more quickly and effectively. Most of the time.

* * *

When Delegation Doesn't Work Out

Sometimes an attempt at delegation bombs. Deborah reflected, "There's gonna be times when people disappoint you." She recognized that it can be frustrating when you've given a project to someone else and that person leaves or doesn't follow through in the way you'd wish. Especially when it puts the task back on your desk.

When that happens, Deborah suggested, "If you try to view all the tasks that have to be done as things that are important to the business' success then it feels a lot less tedious when you have to take it back."

One time, one of her clients moved to a new website platform and tags needed to be added to products so that they could be found when someone searched their store. The hammers needed hammer tags and the power drills needed power drill tags, whatever words a customer would use to search for the product. She split the task between two staffers and thought it was handled.

Except, it never seemed to get done. "I had to remind them and remind them," she said. "And then when I finally got it back it was a complete and total disaster. It was all wrong and I had to redo all the work."

She was exasperated. But did her best to use the opportunity to re-educate the staffers about what needed to be done and why. The trouble was that one person was a short-timer who was about to leave the company, so they didn't care too much.

Any time you delegate and it doesn't work out, it leads to questions of, "What could I have done to improve how that may have gone?" she said. For some when this happens they get frustrated and give up, thinking they hate managing people and suck at it. When in reality, missteps happen even to experienced managers. It's a great opportunity to learn to trust your own intuition and use your best communication skills.

Have a gut feeling that the person doesn't know which end is up? Don't leave that alone and walk away. Address it or it will come back to bite you later.

Remember that even experienced delegators don't do it perfectly. If you get frustrated and close the door on welcoming support, achieving more will be much harder, if not impossible.

* * *

Explain Why Tasks You Delegate Matter

Deborah explained how important it is for the person receiving the work to understand how the tasks they're doing fit into the whole business. The better they understand this, the more capable and effective they can be at doing it. It also shifts that task from just something random and tedious and helps them take ownership of how they're making a direct impact in your organization. This increases their engagement.

She said in her own experience when things didn't work out, "had I spent maybe fifteen minutes taking the time to do that explanation [of how the task fit into the greater whole], things would've gone a lot better."

I asked her what she wished she would've known when she started managing people. Her answer surprised me.

"I wish I would've known that people for the most part actually don't mind that you're giving them work." She continued, "And just because I think it's a little boring and tedious doesn't mean I should have to do it because it's not fair to someone else [to have to do something boring and tedious]."

She said the key was focusing on the big picture. What benefited the company most was making sure she was using her highest level skills and letting others do things that were suited to their skill sets.

* * *

DECIDING WHAT TO DELEGATE

Choosing what to delegate and where to get support can be tricky. Deborah said when she looks at the things that need to get completed in any day, "I first break things into activities that I really really like and things I don't like quite as much."

Next, she thinks about which projects required senior level experience to handle and which could be handled by someone with less experience. Between those two lists it is pretty easy for her to determine which things to hand off to others.

If there was anything on the list that a particular employee would be excited about doing, she recommends giving them the opportunity. "Let them take it. You're going to have even more space to do things will grow revenue and grow your business even more. They will do a good job at it because it interests them."

* * *

TRANSFER RESPONSIBILITIES NOT TASKS

Deborah pointed out that the essential piece in any hand off, "is to educate the person that you're handing it to so that they take ownership of what you've given to them. It's not just a task you've passed to them. It's a responsibility you've passed to them."

She explained the difference between a task and a responsibility like this, "A task is like when mom used to say, 'vacuum.'" On the other hand, a responsibility would be if she'd ask you to help her take care of the house you shared and explained that vacuuming is how you could help her do it. Instead of telling you what to do, she'd need to have a conversation with you as a valuable member of the team and share why what you're doing is important. The difference is mostly in the approach.

Deborah also recommended what she coined as "reverse delegation." Check-in periodically and see if your expertise can help automate activities your team finds extremely tedious.

* * *

It's Okay to Ask for Help

Remember, as a leader the trickle down follows from you. Whatever you model personally in your family or professionally in your work is an example for everyone else to follow about what is acceptable. If you try to do everything yourself and don't ask for help even when you need it, your family or team will likely follow the same patterns for better or for worse.

REFLECT:

Where are you doing a great job of welcoming support personally and professionally?

Where is there opportunity for you to welcome in even more support?

How would this allow you to achieve your personal or professional goals more quickly or enjoy your life more?

What do you tell yourself that keeps you from welcoming support that is already available to you?

IMPLEMENT:

What one step are you committed to taking this week to begin allowing in even more support personally or professionally?

To avoid burn out while
upleveling your impact
you must also uplevel
your support.

THE S.A.S.S. SYSTEM:

SYSTEMIZED

CHAPTER THIRTEEN:

IMPLEMENT SYSTEMS THAT SUPPORT FREEDOM & SCALABILITY

I DIDN'T USED TO THINK THAT STRUCTURE WAS SEXY. The idea of committing to systemizing more parts of my life and work felt constraining and limited, the opposite of freedom.

My schedule was completely variable. I got up when I wanted. I went to bed when I wanted. I ate when I felt like it. I worked when I wanted. That was what I thought freedom looked like.

Though the result was my work was erratic. My mood was all over the place. My income was all over the place. I felt like I was working all the time even when I wasn't really. I'd space out and forget appointments. I consistently broke agreements with myself and others.

Let's face it, going completely structure-free doesn't work unless the goal is chaos, inconsistency, and flakiness. That wasn't mine.

Turns out, it's not just kids that thrive when there's structure—adults do too. And though I've seen the positive results of embracing that structure in my own life, admittedly that still doesn't mean that I'm 100% on board.

Even now there are days the rebel inside of me just doesn't feel like following the rules, even my own. And sometimes I don't. When I do this usually what happens is that I pay the consequences later, creating more work for myself or seeing a door close on an opportunity.

I've found the more I give attention to the processes that create more of what I want and do more of those, the better results I'm able to achieve. It also sets me up to better leverage my time and more easily receive help from others.

* * *

WHY SYSTEMS?

A system is a process designed to achieve a particular result. When you implement them well personally and professionally they improve your efficiency and reduce decision fatigue. If you have staff, you absolutely need effective systems to create consistent results so your processes can be run without you being present.

Much of our lives and work consist of tasks we do over and over. And naturally, when we figure out something that works well, we often continue to do the same routine without even realizing it.

You probably have systems you're already using that you may not have identified as such. A system can be as simple as the consistent way you start your morning so that you have a productive day. You might have a system for how you make decisions. You might have a system for how you organize your home or work space or car or computer. You probably have a system for how you hire a babysitter or other staff. When you have a system for doing things and don't realize it, particularly when you have others working for you, this can lead to a ton of frustration and miscommunication.

* * *

Communication is the Key to Systems Creating Freedom

Cathy, one of my clients and vice-president at a billion dollar tech company, had hired a personal assistant. Part of the assistant's work was to do some household chores including laundry. And Cathy was constantly frustrated with the way her assistant did this part of her job.

Things were never folded correctly. The kids clothes weren't put away in their rooms. Towels were distributed in the wrong bathrooms. Sometimes even a whole load of clothes would wind up dyed the wrong color.

It seemed ridiculous to Cathy that she should need to train someone on how to do laundry. When we talked about it she asked me, "Wasn't this something that everyone learned as a teen?" Clearly based on the results she had been getting, no, not everyone had learned how to do laundry as a teen.

And that's exactly the point. Because everyone's experience and context are different, we need to formally create and communicate our systems so that regardless of someone's previous experience or how they are socialized they can deliver the end result we have in mind. In this case, that meant keeping the whites white and the blue towels in the downstairs bathroom.

So Cathy agreed to formalize the system by breaking it down into steps starting with sorting the laundry into like colors, which settings to use on the washing machine with how much detergent, which things went in the dryer and which didn't, how she wanted things folded, and where different items got put away.

And, by formalizing and documenting her system, not only did Cathy get what she wanted from her assistant, she also could have anyone else fill in and still get things done in exactly the same way every time. That helped Cathy leverage her time more effectively so she could focus on other things. It also dramatically reduced her frustration.

Often, we don't formalize our systems when it would be helpful to do so. Without formalization even on a system we use on our own, it can be easy to inadvertently miss a step without noticing.

When you have things formalized, you can follow a checklist of steps each time you do something. Nothing gets missed.

And when you aren't getting the results you'd like in your life or work it becomes easy to see which step has been forgotten or needs tweaking to get the desired result. No need to recreate the wheel.

* * *

WHERE TO START WITH SYSTEMS?

First, the place I usually suggest clients start is to look for where in their life or work do they seem to be wasting time or consistently frustrated over the same things? Make a list of those things, then begin by focusing on the one or two that if they were resolved would be the greatest relief or impact.

Another of my clients, Johanna, owner of a high-end spa, said one of her main stressors was with clients cancelling their appointments within the 24-hour no cancellation window. Because she didn't have a good system for how she dealt with this, it was a major frustration and opportunity loss because she couldn't fill the appointments even with a waiting list.

Even though she officially had a late-cancellation fee, she never charged it because she didn't want to be perceived as a hard ball who didn't care and risk having clients go somewhere else. The adjusted policy and system for tracking this dramatically reduced the problem. Her stress decreased, and her income went up because she was dealing with it consistently.

What she did was have each new client initial on their intake form that they understood the new policy. If they cancelled within 24 hours of their appointment or no-showed, they would be billed the full value of their appointment as a cancellation fee. Existing clients were asked to sign that they understood and agreed to the policy at their next appointment and the form was added to their file.

From that point, if a client cancelled a session within the 24-hour window prior to their appointment, all Johanna or any of her staff had to do was look in the file to see whether the client had signed an acknowledgement of the policy already.

Either way, she waived the fee the first time and reminded them of the policy, letting them know that this was the only time they would get a freebie. She then added a note that they had received their one fee waiver to their file so if it happened again she would have record of it.

Johanna felt great about this solution because it put her in the position of being compassionate, yet professional. And as a result, she stopped having any problem clients who regularly cancelled at the last minute.

Effective systems implemented consistently solve problems, plain and simple. It's really about getting clear about what result you're looking for and then building in the steps that will consistently deliver that result in a way that is scalable.

In the example I just mentioned, the spa owner wanted to discourage last minute cancellations and make sure she and her staff were still getting paid because last minute openings often couldn't be filled. Her system addressed both issues well. And the consistent documentation meant that anyone on her team could follow the same protocol even on the owner's days off.

By developing processes that do not require you to be present, you can delegate and leverage your time. That way growth can happen in ways that do not limit your personal freedom.

* * *

ESSENTIAL SYSTEMS FOR EVERYONE

There are two systems that I've personally found are essential to staying energized and far away from burn out. My clients adopt their personal versions:

1. Mindful Morning Routine.

2. Sustainable Work Scheduling.

Mindful Morning Routine:

Objective:
Create an upbeat, productive mindset focused and ready to complete my most important tasks of the day.

The Routine:
My morning starts waking up with my sunrise simulator alarm clock weekdays at 7:45 a.m. I was completely resistant to waking up by alarm because I had always associated it with slave labor of working for *the man*. The trouble was, after moving to Minneapolis, in the dark of winter my natural body clock preferred that I sleep until ten in the morning or later.

Using this alarm clock that starts gradually making the room light fifteen minutes before my wake-up time, I'm able to wake up gently at a much earlier time without any abrupt shock. This has been a major upgrade to my routine since this is my least favorite part of day and mornings have consistently been tough for me.

I sit in bed and do some meditation, focus on my mission and affirmations and do some visualization with my vision board. Mindfulness is followed by breakfast. This needs to be part of my system because eating is something I historically have forgotten to do.

Next comes beautifying. First, beautifying my space. Without this I'm really good at letting clutter get out of hand and cleaning at the end of the day isn't my thing. So I pick one thing whether that's doing dishes or picking up clothes or filing papers from the day before and tackle it. Ten minutes and it's done and I already feel productive.

Next is beautifying me. A shower has me feeling bright and lively. Admittedly, if I don't have plans to meet with anyone, sometimes I skip this step.

Only then is it time for work. I start work with my highest priority task for the day. I find that when I skip any of these steps my day doesn't go as well as those when I do each of these. Am I perfect about it? No. Yet I do it consistently more often than I don't because I know it puts me in a great state to have a wonderful day.

Sustainable Work Scheduling:

Objective: Identify specific, regular times for work, rest, and fun so that I stay healthy, balanced, and effective.

The Schedule that Works for Me:
I build my work calendar so that I ease in and ease out of my work week. I do better this way without abrupt starts and stops.

When I work five days a week (I don't always), Mondays are project and strategy days. I can work on my business instead of in my business. Tuesday through Thursday I see clients 10:00 a.m.–5:00 p.m. By 7:00 p.m. every night work is done, and I am onto relaxing and having fun doing other things. Friday morning are also project days and the day I handle any finance issues. Saturday and Sunday are fun days and I don't do any work unless I'm attending an event or have scheduled time to work on a big project (like writing this book).

* * *

Systemize From Frustration to Freedom
There are many systems that you're probably using in your work and life both consciously and unconsciously. When you start to notice patterns where things consistently do not deliver the result you are after, look at the system you are using and see what is missing. If you don't have a system, create one.

REFLECT:

Where in your life or work do you seem to be wasting time or consistently frustrated over the same things? Make a list.

Now of the items on the list, which one would be the one that would make the biggest impact for you if it was resolved?

What result would you like to see consistently around this issue?

What would be the impact of achieving this? How could it help you or others?

IMPLEMENT:

What first step are you committed to taking this week to begin systemizing this issue?

Systemize your Sanity.

CHAPTER FOURTEEN:

DOCUMENT YOUR SYSTEMS & KNOWLEDGE

I was debating. I had a ton of work to do, and my partner and I had planned to go camping over Labor Day weekend. I wasn't sure how I was going to get it all done including getting packed for the trip.

The tents, the sleeping bags and mattress, planning the menus, gathering the food—why does prepping for camping always feel like it takes forever??? And why did I always feel as though I do most of that by myself?

It's because that's how I set it up. I was the only one who knew where the gear was and what we needed since the camping stuff was all mine. Even though my partner had been camping with me before, she'd never participated in packing and double-checking we had everything. The check-list for what to bring lived only in my head.

I had created a classic information silo. I was the only one with the information, thus I couldn't easily ask for help or delegate the packing project.

And because I hadn't documented what needed to be packed, what to make sure we had, or where to find everything, I was stuck with doing this task on my own—over and over until I did something differently. This wasn't working.

There are tons of things we do this way in our life and work. We could easily get help if we had a better way to share the information and processes that exist only in our heads.

I bet there is something that you'd love to get help with in your personal or professional life—something that you have a system for doing it. But because you don't have a way to easily share your system with someone else, you just keep doing it over and over again on your own.

* * *

THE VALUE OF DOCUMENTATION

It turns out that it barely matters if you have a system for something if it's not documented. Because you'll always keep bumping up against the limits of what you can do on your own.

If you're looking for scalability, if you're looking to feel more supported by people around you, if you'd like to be able to focus your time and energy on the high level tasks that truly only you can do, then you need to get your systems out of your head. Document them in a way you can share your processes easily so someone else can help.

Because if it's not documented you can't easily hand of that task. And further, if whomever normally handles something is sick, delayed, or unavailable, nobody else can fill in seamlessly while they are gone.

So if you want to do life and work with less stress you'll need to document your systems both personally and professionally so you can get help *and* get consistent results. The same strategies apply whether that's loading new toner into the copier, onboarding a new client, fixing the kids lunch, or packing gear for a camping trip.

* * *

Getting Started Documenting Your Systems

In the case of my camping trip, I needed to document my system for collecting all the things needed so that they could be gathered and packed by someone else without forgetting anything.

I'm going to walk you through exactly how I made explainer videos to do this so that you can do the same with your own systems that live in your head.

Step 1:
Choose the way you will document your system.

There are many ways you can document a system. There is no one right way, it's a matter of choosing the way that will work best for the process you are documenting.

Sometimes, a simple **checklist** is enough. If that's all you need, then for goodness sake don't over complicate things. Just make the checklist and be done with it.

You can write **step-by-step instructions** out without any visuals. I generally don't recommend this way if you have another choice. Following a detailed instruction manual can be tedious—both to create it *and* to use it. Does anyone read a user manual these days? Only if they have to so go this route only if it's absolutely necessary.

Better would be to **take pictures of the steps and write captions** for each step or activity. This is definitely a better option than writing out detailed instructions.

But the easiest to both create and use is a **short explainer video for each step**. Whether it's personal or work, most of us would rather watch a couple minute video about how to do something rather than read about it in a boring manual. This is especially the case if you will be delegating to a young person.

Whenever possible, videos are a great solution to easily walk someone through the steps that are in your head. Note that the videos do not need to be production quality. You can take them easily on your phone. If they're only for an internal audience you can leave them rough and unedited. It's more important that it's done and the information is documented.

In my case, because I needed someone to be able to visually identify the items that were being packed for the camping trip, I opted for video. A checklist may be added later as a backup, but the video was essential for explaining what the items looked like and what needed to be double-checked about each of them.

STEP 2:

BREAK THE PROJECT INTO PARTS OR SEQUENTIAL STEPS THAT A 10-YEAR-OLD COULD EASILY FOLLOW.

Keep things simple. If you need a college degree to understand the instructions, you will fail at getting consistent results. Create the plan for communicating the directions so that a 10-year-old without any experience can be successful at doing what you had in mind.

If you personally get consistent results with something, there *is* a system that you follow even if you don't know it consciously. To pull it out of your head, slow down and think about the first bite sized piece of what you do first. Then second, then third, continuing until you get to the end of the process.

If you're writing the script for how to answer the phone at your office, the first step might be to say, "Hello, thank you for calling Fuller Accounting, how may I help you?" The second step might be, listen to what the person says. The third step might be three options depending on how the person calling responds. Each option might have it's own instructions.

Packing for camping isn't so much sequential as it is about packing different kinds of things. So the way that I chose to break it down into parts was into one video about tents, sleeping gear, and personal items. Another video focused on food and cooking gear. Then a final one covered clothing. That way, each video could be three to five minutes and nothing would be overwhelming. Implementing this it would be easy for someone to watch one video and pack one category of items before moving onto the next.

STEP 3:

DO ANY PREP NEEDED TO CLEARLY COMMUNICATE THE STEPS IN THE PHOTO OR VIDEOS.

If I was teaching someone how to make cupcakes in a particular way, it makes sense to pre-prepare cupcakes in the various stages so you have ones already done to show. This way you can zip through the instructions on the videos.

So in this example you'd have one cupcake in the pan with the raw dough before it is baked. One cupcake would be baked but not frosted, another after it's been frosted. And finally, the last one would have the decorations on top of the frosting completed.

For my packing project, I laid all the gear out on the bed and couch so it could be easily seen and I could flow seamlessly from one type of gear to the next.

I could've laid the stuff out for each video separately, shot the video, then laid out the next grouping of things and shot that video. It seemed more efficient to me to lay everything out all at once and then shoot all the videos one after another. Do whatever makes the most sense to you depending on what you are intending to show.

STEP 4:
SHOOT THE VIDEOS

Using your phone, shoot short videos while you talk out loud through the steps and process you follow for this activity. Show as much as you can instead of just telling.

Be clear and direct, keeping things simple. Remember, a 10-year-old needs to be able to follow you for this to be successful.

Don't worry about hair or make-up or getting all the words right. This is only about getting it done. You don't need to script anything in advance, just talk normally as if the person who will be doing the process is standing right next to you.

If you can do a show and tell through the entire process clearly in only 3–5 minutes, that can be its own video. If you need a few minutes for each step, for ease and clarity, separate each step into its own video.

In my camping packing videos I missed a few things the first time out. A blanket I expected to be in a bag wasn't. There were things that were missing from my kitchen kit. No need to get it perfect. I continued on and made sure I filmed these later so I could add those parts onto original videos.

STEP 5:
SHARE THE VIDEOS

The simplest way I've found to share videos is to drop them into a folder on Google Drive that's named well so I know what it is. Wherever you typically share files will do. In my case, my videos went into a folder called "Packing for

Camping." Then I can share that folder with any person I want to help me and they will have full access to everything that is inside.

STEP 6:
HAVE SOMEONE ELSE FOLLOW THE INSTRUCTIONS TO TEST YOUR DOCUMENTATION

This is straight forward. You give whomever you're asking to help you access to the instructions you've created and have them follow them.

In my case, that will be having my partner prepare for the next camping trip on her own. Yes, sometimes the testing phase involves some faith. It can be a bit bumpy in the transition depending on how well you articulate the instructions and how detail-oriented the person following them is.

If the person does something unexpected or incorrectly based on what you had in mind, then know that there is something that needs adjustment about your instructions. They are not to be blamed for doing something incorrectly, it's an opportunity for you to refine the instructions for your process.

STEP 7:
MAKE ANY ADJUSTMENTS TO THE INSTRUCTIONS AND THEN REPEAT STEP 6 UNTIL YOU CONSISTENTLY GET THE DESIRED RESULT.

* * *

INCLUDE YOUR TEAM IN DOCUMENTING THEIR SYSTEMS

Many times in a business a system or process might be handled by someone on your team. What happens if they leave, get sick, or go on vacation? Will others be able to easily pick up their task list?

Sure, you might have a big training manual—but when was the last time you used it or updated it?

This is an easy issue to solve if you can have each person do explainer videos with their phone for their essential tasks. That way even without a complex manual, you'd be able to easily train someone else to do what they're doing if the person whose job it normally is leaves, has a heath scare, or is on vacation.

In addition to their essential work processes based on their role, also have them explain their filing system, where to find things on their computer, and which software or equipment is used for which tasks. If they do one two-minute video every day for a month, you'll have as many as twenty videos in thirty days on how to do the components of their job.

This will also enable your team to better cover for one another when they go on vacation. Everyone wins when after a vacation someone doesn't come back to a pile of work on their desk and email box. If you have people cross-trained in different roles then the essentials still get done. Employees returning from a break can ease back into work instead of getting slammed in the face when they walk back in the door.

* * *

The Freedom is in the Documentation

I'll admit that documenting even a simple system can be time consuming. But think of all the extra time, money, and energy you'll save long-term by having the option of delegating to others, always having backup at the ready, and by getting consistent results even with newer members of your team.

Documenting your systems in ways that are easy for people to follow is the key to experiencing freedom and allowing more support into your life both personally and professionally.

REFLECT:

What is one place you consciously use a system personally or professionally but you can't delegate the activity to someone else because it only lives in your head?

What would be the best way to document the system so it can be referenced by someone else? Written directions? Pictures? Video? A Checklist? Something else?

How would documenting this entire system support other aspects of your life and/or work?

Quickly list the steps or components that are part of the system or process you use.

IMPLEMENT:

What commitment are you willing to make about completing the documentation of this system so that you have the option to delegate it?

NOBODY ELSE CAN
ACCESS A SYSTEM IN YOUR
HEAD EXCEPT YOU.

DOCUMENT TO DELEGATE.

CHAPTER FIFTEEN:

ALLOW YOUR PLANS & SYSTEMS TO EVOLVE

AFTER MONTHS OF AN UNFRUITFUL JOB SEARCH IN A DOWN economy in Portland, Oregon, in early 2001, Jennifer Martin, now of Zest Business Consulting, decided on a different tactic. She would buy a business and run it herself.

She'd done the research and narrowed the field, eventually settling on a small restaurant in a trendy Northwest District. The business was losing money every month, but after looking at their business model which focused on a walk-in lunch clientele, with her sales and marketing background she saw there were opportunities for growth.

"I expected that I would go in, make some changes and in six months I'd turn around and sell it at a profit," said Jennifer. They had menus that worked, many systems that made sense, a staff that knew what they were doing, appealing branding, and a physical space that was already complete. It was something to build on that didn't require starting from scratch. So she negotiated the deal and on August 28, 2001, escrow closed and she was the proud owner of a restaurant.

She began rolling out her plans and getting to know staff and customers. Everything looked on track until two weeks later, September 11th hit. The next day, not one customer came into the restaurant. Or the next day. Or the day after that.

"It was as if a bomb went off in Portland. People were scared to go out of the house," she recalled.

All the plans she had for turning around the restaurant and getting out quickly went up in smoke that day. In an instant the business went from losing a few hundred a month to losing thousands.

"All my plans had to change, no one was going to restaurants any more. Mine wasn't the only one that was empty. I had to make changes and I had to do it fast or I wasn't going to be in business very long."

She scratched her original strategy to add seating and open for dinner and focused on seeking business in the only place people were still spending money on food: corporate catering.

"Law firms and pharmaceutical reps catering lunches for high end clients became my biggest customers. If I'd gone with the original strategy I planned I would've been bankrupt in two months."

The changes and places she had to scale back to stay in business didn't make her very popular with staff. One of these changes was in the way they made their signature brownies. The original version used premium ingredients and required the chef to hand shave chocolate as part of the recipe. It was a source of pride for the restaurant, though to make money they had to sell each one for at least $5 or more with labor.

So Jennifer ran taste tests with a version of brownie using a bulk package from the supermarket with extra chocolate chips thrown in it. Customers loved them. And at $3 per brownie they became a highly profitable, top-selling item.

The chef felt this downgraded the food and insulted her work. She also didn't like that Jennifer had streamlined the chef's hours because the restaurant wasn't making enough money to pay her when the same work could be done by lower wage staff.

The disagreements escalated and the chef eventually left in a huff without notice. She walked out the day before the restaurant was to deliver fifty turkeys and Thanksgiving fixings for the November holidays.

Fortunately, things didn't fall apart with the chef's departure. Jennifer picked up the slack and delivered delicious food to customers on time.

The surprise was that what Jennifer had thought was holding the ship together was actually making it more difficult to steer in a new direction. The original chef was attached to doing things the old way far more than she was to making a profit and selling what customers would buy in a tough market.

With that resistance to change removed, Jennifer was able to re-evaluate and shift their approach to business. She moved quickly to adjust the systems they were using. Her whole business model became about responding to what clients wanted and offering what they were willing and interested in buying.

Jennifer recalled, "It seemed like at this time in Portland another restaurant closed their doors every day. But by being flexible and responding to changes in the market we were able to stay afloat and eventually get in the black. I was finally sell the business at a profit as I originally intended—it just took longer than six months."

What to Do When Things Stop Working

It can be that systems work great, delivering fantastic results up until the moment when they don't. Sometimes this is because something in the market has changed. Sometimes it's because we have changed or grown. Sometimes different employees require something new.

The new normal can happen gradually. Other times, it's similar to Jennifer's story where one day something works and the next day suddenly everything is different.

Once we notice something isn't working it's up to us to make the shift. The sooner we're willing to do that, the easier it can be. When we choose to be attached to doing things the same way—focusing on sameness of process over sameness of results, that's when we can get stuck.

If customers will buy a $5 hand-shaved chocolate brownie, great. As soon as they don't, how can you sell a $3 brownie that's faster to make that they like more?

If your morning routine suddenly isn't leaving you feeling focused, positive, and productive, what needs to be adjusted so that it works again?

* * *

Avoid Jumping to Conclusions & Get Curious

Asking the right questions will help you to determine what needs to be adjusted in your plans and systems. Without any further investigation Jennifer could've decided that clients didn't like brownies anymore when they stopped buying the $5 batches.

Instead, she got curious and found out they still love brownies, customers just couldn't justify the price tag when they were worried about whether they'd have a job the following month. Reducing labor and materials cost was how the system for brownies needed to be adjusted. The end result delivered a less costly brownie that could profitably be sold at a price people would buy it.

* * *

EVOLVE OR DIE

If you look at transportation, a system that is designed to transport goods 2,000 miles with a fuel cost of $4 per gallon may not work when gas escalates to $10 or $20 per gallon. Any company that doesn't make the adjustment will be out of business as the rest of the world evolves.

Recognize the trends, be flexible, and make the adjustments personally and professionally when something becomes unsustainable *or* when it is no longer aligned for you. And if you happen to discover a better way than how you've been doing things, make space for the upgrade!

* * *

LISTEN WHEN THOSE AROUND YOU ARE ASKING FOR CHANGE

I was in a training program for some time where my mentor had been using some technology for the calls that did not allow the participants to see one another even though we were having conversations and doing activities together.

Those of us on the calls found this very frustrating and cumbersome as interacting with one another required having the facilitator mute and unmute group members to speak. There was not any organic flow to the conversation.

A few of us had experience with a service that for $10 a month allowed a large group of people to all participate in video calls together. Having group calls with live video feeds allowed for intimacy as if we were all in the room together.

We asked our mentor to switch systems so we would all have a better experience.

In the beginning he said he would look into it. Eventually, he insisted the new technology could not be integrated and automated into the systems he was already using. He was prioritizing his process over the experience of the people he was serving. This didn't make any of us very happy.

A few months went by where he continued to stonewall even though half the group wanted the switch to be made because we were using this other technology in our own groups and we loved it.

Finally, he relented and made the transition. Once he switched it turned out he loved the new system. He was delighted with how much more interactive the calls could be and how much deeper of a connection everyone made when we could see one another face-to-face. By changing systems he got much better results from the calls and his clients (us) were more satisfied.

When we hold tight to how we've been doing things even when we're presented with a better alternative, we wind up wasting more time and delaying movement into more ease and effectiveness.

Focus on the results of what you're looking to create, then decide what needs to happen in order to create that result. Evolution is the name of the game.

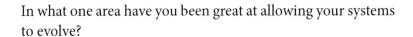

REFLECT:

In what one area have you been great at allowing your systems to evolve?

In what one area have you continued doing things the way you've always done even if you're not getting the results you want?

How might you consider approaching this issue differently?

IMPLEMENT:

What is one step you're committed to taking personally or professionally this week to adjust a system or plan so that it fits better with what's happening right now?

Things change. Life happens. Markets shift. People grow.

Be open to adjusting how you're doing things to suit the new normal.

THE S.A.S.S. SYSTEM:

WHERE TO GO FROM HERE

CHAPTER SIXTEEN:

INTEGRATION & NEXT STEPS

CHANGING LIFELONG PATTERNS TAKES TIME. AND WE'RE talking more than the 21–90 days experts speculate it takes to make a new habit automatic. In the absence of support our natural tendency is to revert back to what we're most comfortable with—our old patterns.

Most women struggle implementing these concepts long-term while still living in an environment that hasn't changed. What do you do when other people expect you to behave a certain way and you no longer do? When your partner, family, or team aren't supportive? What do you do when you hit a roadblock or doubt yourself as you step out from the status quo? What do you do when the itty bitty shitty committee in your head can't be silenced?

Going it on your own is hard, lonely, and anything but fun. You already know that story because like me, you've spent most of your life doing it: proving you didn't need anyone else. Yet at the same time, wishing to belong to a community.

Living and working with S.A.S.S. is an ongoing conversation. So every situation you encounter provides a new opportunity to actively design your life and work using this philosophy.

* * *

Uplevel Your Environment with Greater Support

Making the shift permanent is almost guaranteed when you have the close ongoing support of like-minded high achieving women who are affirming cheerleaders of your new choices. Women who reject that self-sacrifice and feeling drained and burned out is the only way to achieve. Women just like you who are bringing their big vision to life while actively staying focused on what really matters: joy, happiness, health, and having quality time with people they love.

Imagine making new choices and rolling them out in your life within a community of ten sisters who know and love you. Women who see your brilliance and value and remind you when you forget. Women who are trusted advisors that will tell you the truth even if it's hard to say.

Women who are leaders just like you that understand making difficult choices and being pulled in many directions all at once. Those who encourage you to say YES to yourself. Deeply committed friends who you can call on the phone or send a text message when you get stuck. Women who want you to achieve your goals as much as they want achieve their own. Women who recognize that together is better.

You'll find this level of support and community in my elite mastermind: *The High Achiever's Haven.*

I don't believe in a one-size-fits-all approach and *The High Achiever's Haven* isn't right for everyone. It's only for women who are achieving at the highest levels and committed to giving themselves guilt-free permission to relax, live passionately, and enjoy life too.

Other options for upleveling your environment with support could include joining me for:

- Restorative retreats with other high achieving women.

- My boundary-setting bootcamp, *Say NO Like a Pro.*

- One-on-one mentoring going deeper into aspects where you need more guidance which could include:
  - *Saying goodbye to guilt.*
  - *Designing and implementing a plan so you can confidently take a work-free vacation without your cell phone.*
  - *Implementing the S.A.S.S. System in any area of your life or work.*

GET YOUR FREE CUSTOM PLAN TO UPLEVEL YOUR ENVIRONMENT

To discover whether *The High Achiever's Haven* or any of the other options fit for your unique situation AND walk away with a custom plan to uplevel your environment with greater support on this new path (whether or not you choose to do any further work with us) visit:

WWW.ACHIEVEMORENEXTSTEPS.COM

You'll apply for a complimentary, no obligation *Uplevel Your Environment* call. Once we've reviewed your application and determined that we believe we can help, we'll get you scheduled for the free private session with a member of my team. Go do that now before life (and your environment) get in the way and you're onto the next thing.

* * *

FINAL THOUGHTS

Taking this philosophy further requires deeper engagement, consistent reminders, and a community of sisters who get it. If the concepts in this book have resonated with you, I'd be honored to be your personal mentor. I look forward to continuing to connect with you in the Facebook group and hearing your successes and challenges.

Above all else, remember that living with S.A.S.S. is about being gentle with yourself and taking one day at time. KEEP UP THE GREAT WORK!

* * *

SPREAD THE **YES** TO **LESS** MOVEMENT

If this is a book that's been helpful to you and you want to help other women find it, reviews on Amazon are of significant support. Or, gift this book to your colleagues and friends with your personal recommendation. Thank you!

REFLECT:

In what ways do you need to uplevel your environment with greater support so that you don't bounce back into feeling drained and burned out?

What challenges have you had about finding that support on your own?

What excites you about the idea of having greater support in your life?

IMPLEMENT:

Get your free customized plan to uplevel your environment with greater support on this new path:

www.AchieveMoreNextSteps.com

IN THE ABSENCE OF SUPPORT, ENVIRONMENT ALWAYS WINS.

- JAY FISET

ABOUT THE AUTHOR

AN AWARD-WINNING AUTHOR AND A RECOVERING PERFEC-
tionist herself, Joy Evanns mentors high achieving women—
business owners and executives—who have big visions, yet
they feel drained and burned out.

By learning to say YES to LESS in her own life and in
her former career as a graphic designer for clients including
Fortune 100 companies, Joy eliminated resent from her relationships, increased her income, and healed chronic asthma
and back pain.

She loves travel, trying new restaurants, paddleboarding,
walking, enjoying the arts, board games, and getting massage.

For comments, questions, or interview requests, email:
Joy@AchieveMoreBook.com

Printed in Great Britain
by Amazon

80615357R00130